THE KARATE SENSEI

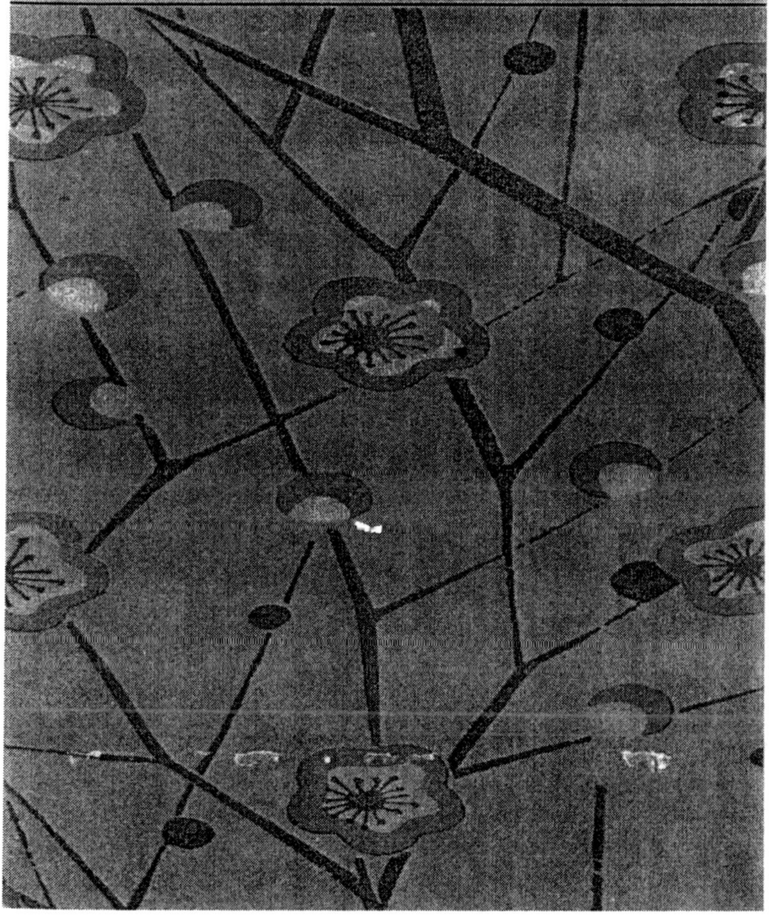

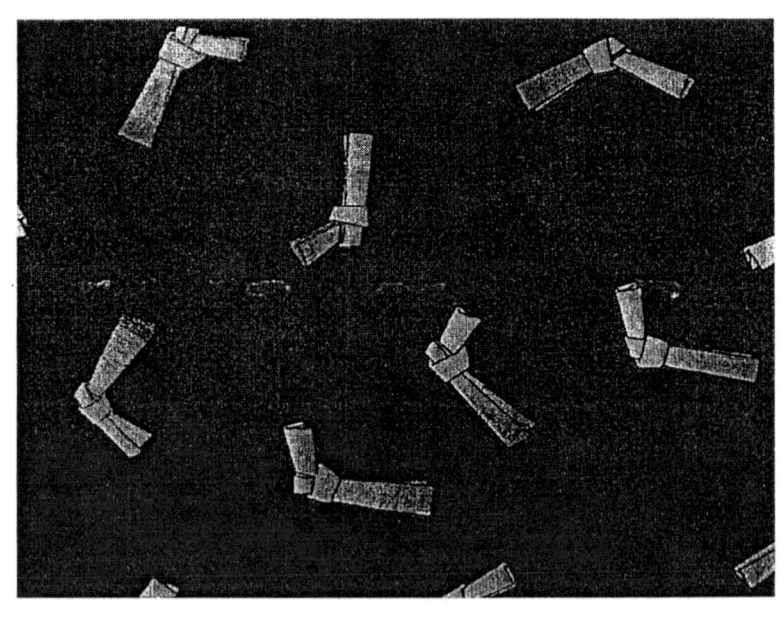

KARATE IS MOTION PLUS EMOTION

Peter Urban

THE KARATE SENSEI

COPY RIGHT - Peter Urban 1984

GRAPHIC DESIGN Annette Hellingrath

ISBN 0-920129-06-4
1st Printing 1984
2nd Printing 1989

ISBN 0-920129-28-5
1st Printing Paperback 2005

Pages 6-16 courtesy of Charles E. Tuttle Company
(taken from 'The Karate Dojo' by Peter Urban)

Other drawings & artwork by Peter Urban

MASTERS PUBLICATION
Hamilton - Ontario - Canada

PRINTED IN CANADA

GOJU MEANS: BLOCK SOFT & HIT HARD

Peter Urban
THE KARATE SENSEI

TODAY IS NOW!

About the Author

Peter Urban is a teacher, writer, organizer, businessman and parent. He believes that 'work continues beyond the cemetery.'

He teaches that 'pleasure comes first in our young age, work comes first in our middle age and routine comes first in our old age.' There is nothing else!

Peter Urban's religion is Karate Zen Buddhist, education is eclectic. Sensei Urban defines Zen as: zeal, energy and nowness.

His hobbies include chess, rhetoric and psychology.

Dedication

I dedicate this book to Sensei Richard Kim of the Zen Bei Butoku-Kai with respect and gratitude.

Contents

Introduction.............9
Confession of a 10th Dan..............15
Twenty-six Case Histories.............97
Conclusions of a 10th Dan.............194

Memorize your katas:
1 The American Teikyoku

If justice is giving a person what he or she deserves then: be sure to remember that karate justice is always swift.

Karate training changes the pecking order of life in our lives, as well as that of all the other people in our lives, in this life.

Karate psychology tells us that the fear of reading is part of the fear of learning.

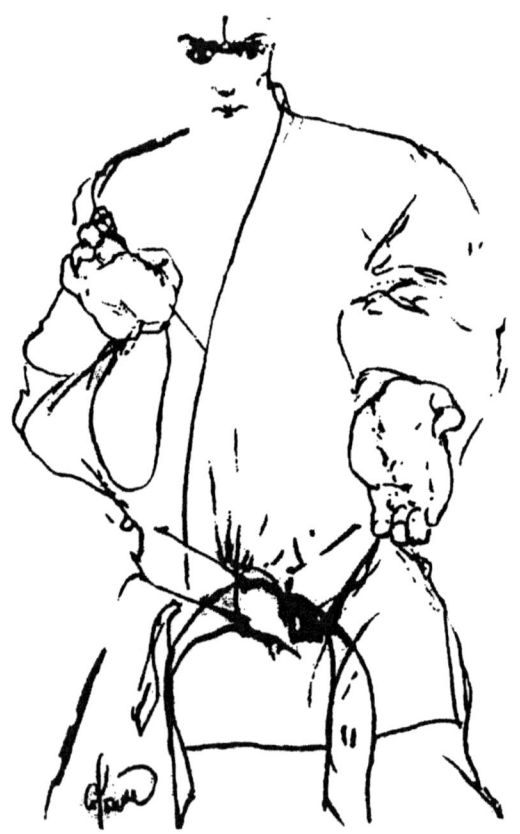

Remember: The essence of confidence is over kill over skill! Confidence is a feeling. It is not an efficient feeling. It is a sufficient feeling.

Practice your katas every day:
2 The American Tenshoa

Remember:
Dreams come true only when the dreaming part has stopped.

Karate psychology teaches us why we cannot be our real selves until we have learned how to fight real good.

Remember: The here and now = Zero.
The there and then = The square root of infinity.
The here to come = Infinity squared.

Perfect your katas:
3 The American Empi-ha

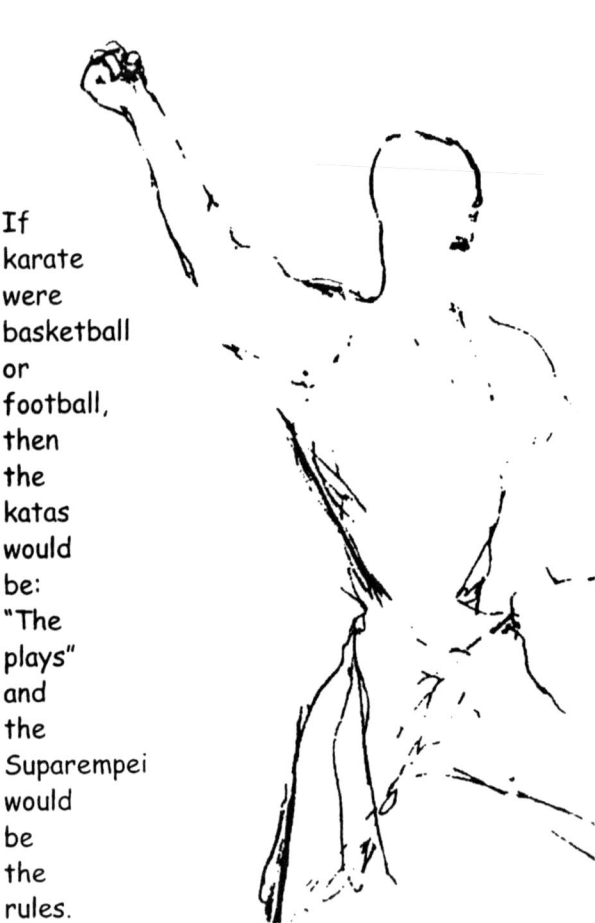

If karate were basketball or football, then the katas would be: "The plays" and the Suparempei would be the rules.

Karate psychology introduces us to a few new words such as "shunting" and the abbreviation "CW" our lives are never the same after that.

Remember: Shakespeare knew exactly the same kata you and I do. To wit, the 26 letters of the English alphabet. The rest was up to him.

Understand your katas:
4 The American Kooroorunfa

Your religion is
anything you do
every day that works
good for you and others
all the time.

Karate
psychology
concerns
itself
with
the why and
how of human
confidence
feelings.

Remember: Karate is really a way of life. It even qualifies as a religion.

Respect your katas:
5 The American Bo-Staff

Karate psychology is taught in a school called a dojo by a teacher called a Sensei.

The Japanese Karate word kata, itself means (way of doing things properly) or "technology."

Remember: Any child who reads any book on electricity today, knows more about electricity than Benjamin Franklin knew in his whole lifetime.

We are our katas:
6 The American Suparempei

The reason people don't mess around with karate people is because the karate people of this world all have a very unique mentality that their enemies know all too well, to wit: "A head for an eye, a heart for a tooth and a tribe for a life."

Karate psychology is my view of human behavior.

The Japanese call the term for that mentality "I-oo-chi." (Iouchi) This is a splendid term for you to commit to memory, in English we usually say "Make 'em pay the price" or "Take 'em with you." That was done a lot in Okinawa and Vietnam by Karate people.

Remember: The book of life is brief, don't skip a page or even a word of it.

Introduction

In the beginning there was the unknown. Fear came before knowledge. A self-defense mechanism is integral to the life potential of all life. Karate is an education, a therapy and an awareness that deals primarily with learning 'how to fight real good.'

The behavior and interactions of all people can be directly related to their ability to fight, to fight back, to preserve and or improve their lives, as well as prolong its existence in the here and now of the accurate world.

I define the word fight as an 'unpleasant emotional experience.' The lack of the knowledge of how to fight real good is the first ignorance responsible for unnatural death, pain, misery, poverty, depression, embarrassment, degradation, rape, shame, suicide, slavery and or subjugation to a host of real and imaginary unpleasant emotional experiences at any time in any life.

This book shall emphasize the important usefulness of one of the limitless numbers of defense mechanisms exhibited in the consideration of all human behavior, to wit, karate training and philosophical-psychoanalysis. It is best done in a school called a dojo and run by a teacher called a Sensei. The rest is style.

I define karate as motion plus emotion. Any classical martial-art with its accompanying philosophical and psychological character building aspects may duly quality as the basic raw materials for the psychological operation of promoting the student up the stairs of accomplishment to the attainment of 'super normalcy' in 'the learning of how to fight really well.' No properly educated lady or gentleman of quality can afford to be without the understanding of their own self-defense mechanisms.

Remember: It is shunting that makes us as people skip baths, meals and payments sometimes. Students and teachers must fight shunting.

EVERYONE WORKS

NOTHING IS FREE

WORK IS THE ROOTS
OF THE TREE OF KNOWLEDGE

These are my findings

Generalities which hold true for individuals hold true for societies. The basic need for a self-defense mechanism is the most obvious common ground that underlies all human behavior. The sex drive itself is one of nature's ways of providing a self defense mechanism for the continuation of the species. I believe that all objects made by man indicate their needs. This holds true for other forms of life as well. A bird's next shows its need for a home.

I have come to accept that neurosis is an internalized psychological mechanism. Neurotic behavior starts when that particular mechanism defends against something unpleasant. It is accepted as a standard operating procedure if it works. This holds true even if it is an example of human fantasy.

People as well as animals are capable of this. I do not yet know if plants and insects can be compared this way or not, but I suspect that such a thing could be quite possible.
Neurosis is any consistency in the face of no longer being apropos, sensible, reasonable, logical or rational behavior. Neurotics make lousy scientists because they stick to things for the sake of it.

Once a neurotic action happens twice, a pattern is planted. It only gets fertilized with repetition of the original reality. Laziness and unnecessary fear are excellent examples of a neurotic reaction to work and to fighting. Procrastination and cowardice behavior modes are taken as acceptable alternatives for the mind energy path to be switched to. I call this "shunting." The amount of energy a person has from moment to moment is a critical factor which ends itself readily to intellectual rationalization for any chosen behavior. The term shunting is my contribution to psychology jargon. Shunting is the opposite of concentrating!

Neurosis is the most common human disease, because non-elective modes of schizophrenia can be forced on people by governments, cultures, or religions. Apartheid, prohibition, mass suicides, and celibacy are examples of this. I define schizophrenia as being one's own shepherd, sheep an wolf at the same time.

Self-therapy is the only therapy in my mind, for the same reason that self-discipline is the only discipline in zen. All therapy of any kind assumes a superiority of the therapist over the rest of the population of humans with a high neurosis rate.

It is because this can not be shown to be true mathematically, all predictions of prophets, all knowledge from teachers, all help from our therapists and teachers, must be viewed with the scientific mind all the time, and the philosophical mind sometimes.

It is necessary to be non-neurotic to view a non-neurotic as a person and not as a machine. Neurosis any consistency! I call this statement "Wright's law." When it is necessary to go beyond the broad generality, I simply and emphatically suffix that statement with the word "sometimes."

The next time you leave your dishes in the sink overnight, ask yourself if you're shunting again or not. Apples fell before Newton, and shunting existed before the term. Let's see what happens in your life as the years go by, now that you know the word. It will be interesting.

Confessions of a Tenth Dan

I, the teacher, confess that I learned my profession by going to my teachers. I mastered my art by teaching it to my students. I crystallized my knowledge by writing about it. I organized me!

I, the author, confess that karate is my way of life.

I, the Sensei, confess that I have learned more from the students than they learned from books. I have heard more words than I have read, and spoken more than I wrote, and thought more than I did. I have listened to more confessions than criticisms.

I, the student, confess that serenity comes from old knowledge, progress comes from new knowledge.

I, the American, confess to being the very first United States tenth-dan professional Sensei in Karate history. This makes me proud.

I like teaching my students to grab the shoulders, punch the face, kick the belly, sweep the legs, hit hard, block soft, feel strong, move swiftly, think straight, breathe like a master and attack implicitly and violently.

My nickname for the devil in us is "the ol' bubonic laziness." I call the will to fail sin.

I call poverty sin. I call shunting retardation. Shunting is nothing new, only the name is. I say that we all shunt until it is pointed out to us. Shunting is feeling one thing and doing another. Shunting is squeezing the trigger on your rifle and blinking the eyes and jerking the face away at the same time. Shunting is looking away when you're punching them in the face.

In my explanations of the constructions of various self-defense mechanisms, I use the abbreviation CW. It is a psychological "impact term." It means: "circus world" or "showing off." This symbol of mine will soon become standard jargon even outside of psychology talk. The term "Reichian armor" is not as adequate as I would like it to be to accurately express my meaning.

CW is part of most behavioral self-defense mechanisms. It shows up strongly in attitude or vibes and image projecting mannerisms. I find it equally evident in people and dogs.
CW is also used offensively. Its purpose is to awe, deceive, divert, amplify, impress, cover-up, inspire fear, or overwhelm. When done consciously, it is acting in its truest sense. It must be remembered that acting itself, is really how to lie really good.

I teach my students that acting is best technically viewed as improved human behavior. Discipline itself, is acting! When CW is done perfectly, it is highly practiced. CW has the most psychological effect when it is done unconsciously. CW mannerisms that become totally neurotic are really handicaps. Unnecessary CW mannerisms that become totally neurotic are really handicaps. Unnecessary CW is amateurish to say the least.

CW can be used to allure. Without it, boys and girls would never get to meet or know each other. A disco is really one big CW party. That, plus the exercise make for the fun of the whole phenomenon.

DIVERSIONARY TACTICIANS utilize CW quite splendidly. Many people use some form of CW as their main weapon of safety in all their dealings in the outside world. This is not an uncommon neurosis among successful "show-biz people."

All super normal acting is a form of CW offense or defense. Flashy uniforms and thrilling bands are part of an army's CW mechanism. CW = male macho. CW = female femi-po-ism. Excessive or out of place CW is a form of public masturbation. Modesty is definitely better than humility. Humility is a form of CW. Think about that for a couple of months. See what conclusions you come to.

Everyone's confessions must include for "stoicism and hysteria" at some place or another. I have found that stoicism is a form of deliberate male retardation. Hysteria is generally seen as a form of female retardation.

"The sexual revolution has decidedly changed all of that, now all people can be equally retarded." I have found that both behavior modes are not usefully exhibited when one is completely alone. I am convinced that no one acts normally when they know they are on camera or record or "on stage."

CW is used heavily on the telephone. Our telephone voice is our acting voice. It is usually at a safe distance. Remember, an astute observer can get just as much accurate data about us from our voices and tone language, as they can from the real vibes. Vibes (etheric-emanations) do come over the telephone! Our telephones themselves, are self-defense mechanisms.

I, as a proponent of "writing therapy," must often times remind myself of Lao Tsu. He once wrote that: "Writing is simply putting down on paper what one can not say to people."

I like to call hysteria psychic magnificato. We all use it best with an audience. Males display just as much hysteria as females. If you don't believe me, check out the behavior you observe at the two and three hour gas lines each morning. This was a very big thing in 1979.

I have learned that a super normal person is one capable of expressing and feeling the entire range of human motion and emotion. Karate Senseis deal with the concept of practicing and inducing confidence through the attainment of super normalcy. Senseis use a self improvement program on themselves and their students forever. Self improvement is the name of the game for embarking upon any discipline. Karate therapy is really classical Karate training of the highest order.

I have come to believe that the most important thing for all of us in our young age is pleasure. The instant that is no longer the case, we enter psychological middle age. I am further convinced that middle age begins the instant we put work first in our lives.

I call the "born again" feelings, putting the "work ethic first!" That stage is usually the most productive and creative part of most successful people's lives.

Old age, or what the Chinese call "wisdom time," commences when "routine" comes first. Routine itself is a superb self-defense mechanism. It keeps a lot of good souls in isolated and un-thanked jobs from going crazy. Dogs love it. The imprisoned look forward to it. They plan their escapes by it and its inevitability. The elderly and hospitalized count on routine.

The psychology of Karate views life and death themselves, as well as "drastic change of environment" or job circumstances, or anything else profound that you can think of dear reader, as just "ordinary" or "extra ordinary routine." Don't ever forget that.

I see life as that time distance we must traverse between the womb and the tomb. It is important to Karate Senseis to have an adequate self-defense mechanism with an excellent understanding of CW. This is important equipment on that journey. Overkill is the word that best describes the essence of confidence. I teach my artist students to view overkill as quality. I teach my engineer students to view the word overkill as efficiency.

Fear is an important human emotion. It is the strongest negative feedback feeling we have. All living organisms with fear circuits need them for survival. It is important in the real world. An overdose of fear can be just as harmful as an underdose of fear can be lethal.

Fear is best described philosophically as: "The difference between doing and not doing!" It is good to be afraid of being misunderstood if you are a responsible person. It is good to be afraid of making a mistake if you are a surgeon or an accountant.

I believe that it is better to be respected than loved or feared. Fear is useful only when used properly. Imaginary fear is useful only when used properly. Imaginary fear is a real enemy. It is the fear of war in all of us that makes armies for all of us. Fear of poverty is good. Fear of work is bad. Fear of fear is stupid.

Karate Senseis take delight in teaching their students Karate to make them safe; not to make them dangerous! Cowardice is a form of laziness. Laziness is definitely the fear of work. It is the fear of losing that makes chess champions become super normal players. Fear works excellently in making people work harder. It ranks only secondly to ambition.

Karate Question: What do you do with work?

Karate Answer: ATTACK IT!

PERFECTION HAS ITS PRICE!

Remember: In Karate psychology, mind control is self control.

Don't Forget: Anyone who can not control themselves is destined to be controlled by others.

Remember: Worry, superstition and prejudice are forms of shunting things in advance. Insurance, maps and understanding the subject are forms of facting things in advance. Simulation is the art of profiting from experience in advance. That is why industrial engineering is so interesting to everyone. It teaches us how to do that real good.

**BLOCK SOFT, HIT HARD!
WORK HARD! PLAY SOFT.**

I don't believe that confidence is a natural instinct. I also do not believe that the will to fail is a natural instinct. Confidence, (not to be confused with stupidity), is definitely a cultivated thing in us. There are many instinctive fears. Fear of falling is certainly useful to the newborn. I was amazed to learn from my favorite teacher (Channel 13), that even newborn eagles have it.

The criterion of value is usefulness. Fear of fear has never been useful! I love to teach my Karate students that it is easier to stay out of trouble that is is to get out of it, once one is in it. These are the rules of the road on anyone's life highway. It is always good to avoid a collision!

Neurotics love to make a specialty of "the general problem causing process" instead of making a religion out of the "general problem solving process." That is one of the main differences between graduates of sheep school in this world and graduates of shepherds' school. It is fun to view life as one thrilling adventure in "problem solving school." One's personality usually dictates what school of human behavior one chooses for oneself.

I have come to the conclusion that addiction of any kind is the very best examples of the word neurosis being defined as any consistency. Our self-defense mechanisms are as varied as our climates, cultures, educations, willingness to take chances, clothing and religions.

Even a priest or a general feels more vulnerable to physical dangers from others when not properly dressed in vestige or garb. Many policemen who really are afraid of their jobs, never quit or change profession because they literally love their legal gun and badge too much.

The proper professional equipment in the hands of a

professional of any kind is the very best self-defense mechanism in the world. It is good that we view our dentists that way. Our cancer and arthritis therapists must best be viewed that way as well. Our surgeons view our bodies as machines, many of them view God as the designer. I have heard the soul or spirit called the driver. I personally admire all machinery, human and otherwise.

"The power of enough money" and money itself, is the business person's main self-defense mechanism. In the grand final ultimate analysis, nothing beats knowing how to use the first real good; especially when it is clenched with the power of enough money. I teach myself and my students that it is the lack of "enough money" that is the root of most evil. They tell me that "there is never enough money." I tell them, "to a master, there is always enough of everything to do anything one must do."

> It is expected
> that this person will continue
> to develop and succeed
> throughout life
> in the way of karate.

A person who has just lost a family sustaining job, feels that he or she has just lost their only self-defense mechanism against the cold realities of starvation and poverty. I believe that the very existence of welfare offices has prevented many suicides and much crime. There are diversified opinions as to whether or not it is too high a price for society to pay.

There are no perfect societies outside of the insect world. Charity and altruism can foster the development of the "bubonic laziness." There are many things that can destroy the work ethic. Mass neurosis and poverty are quite often seen to be going hand in hand down the boulevards of time in all cultures and times.

Millionaires who have lost everything in the stock market crashes of history, have been known to take swan dives out of high windows in buildings they formerly owned. The primary self-defense mechanism of all peoples, is "to make a good living." The way we survive and the methods we use in everyday and extraordinary life are both learned and contrived.

Hunger induces schizophrenia as well as sadism and ultimately the "terminal bubonic laziness feelings." Hypo-glycemiacs, who won't feed themselves, have logic problems. They do not know that food control is the essence of mind control for the same reasons that fuel control is the essence of machine performance control.

Men and women never really divorce their first wife if he or she can still cook better than everyone else in the accurate world. Food can take men away from women for the same reason that enough money can win a woman away from a man.

A good unit type family model housewife cook needs an audience for the same reason that a good actor or artist does. The kitchen was the first pharmacy. It is the most magical pharmacy in the world of science. A workaholic wife can have as much fun in her kitchen as a workaholic husband can have in his den, or garage, or workshop, or library.

There is enough work in a kitchen, (3 times per day, 7 days per week, 365 days per year), to keep the most sophisticated and efficient workaholic happy. You have to like the work, however, to be good at it. Necessity and time get you to learn to like it. Everyone in their right mind hates to do dishes. A dishwasher owner has the equivalent of servo-mechanism slave power.

Never to be a "workaholic on the marriage bed." You can get more productive work done in that sacred place with an on-the-job training attitude. That goes for both boys and girls.

Remember that workaholics never fight other workaholics, except; when or if they get in the way of each others' work. It is best that way.
I oftentimes ask my new white belt students "What

do you call a women with a loaded gun?" "Sir," is the correct answer! This situation occurs a lot in welfare offices, especially in New York City and the south Bronx.

The best way to fight a weapon is with another weapon. Don't ever forget that! Things like words, voice tones, guns, looks, vibrations, as well as mind states and "certain holidays" can cause normal behavioral patterns to vary. Drugs, alcohol and the crowding of critical distances are famous for this. They are all part of "the general problem causing process." We must all be educated in it and not part of it.

A street fighter is anyone who has had a fight in the street. A subway fight is experienced by anyone having a fight in a subway. A bar fighter, a ghetto fighter, ad-infinitum, are glamorized terms used by youngsters and "self educated fighters." The term 'street fighter" usually covers a multitude of abilities and an equal amount of fear engendering mystique.

Remember, in preaching and acting, volunteered war stories are always followed by a commercial message of one type or another. The general rule of war stories is that the really good ones are of necessity left untold. Heroism lies in simply helping the self when there is nothing else in the first place. There is no doubt about it, cowardice is definitely laziness.

Guts can not be taught as readily as fighting technology. A person with a lot of guts is sager than a person with an abundance of technology. A person with the job of professional marine or police officer definitely knows this. Nothing beats superior guts and superior fighting technology.
The subjects of longevity and thanatology are of a paramount importance in a classical Karate education. I teach that the purpose of medical therapy is to make one well. The purpose of orthodox psycho therapy is to make one whole. The purpose of Karate (when viewed as a therapy), as it is by me, is to make one safer and more confident. The scientific building of prowess and discipline does that job. Prowess without discipline is definitely the same as industry without art, to wit, brutality. The purpose of discipline in Karate, as well as in any educative process, is simply "freedom." There is nothing else!

My lazy students have a terrible time with me because I teach them that the fear of reading and the fear of learning is part of the "fear of work." They all come back to me with heads bowed when they realize for themselves that those words are accurate. By then, they usually have what I call "the green belt mentality." They want to grow straight by then. The symbology of white belts is the same as "diapers." Everyone of us has to go through "toilet training school" from the very beginning of life on this planet.

I am never harsh on my "stupid students." I am always cruel! I teach them that opportunity in life knocks once, and sometimes like the postman, twice, but "never kicks the door down." One of the ancient Greeks said, "there is no task-master like a former slave." They make the best teachers for the youth. There is no other way to become a master anyway.

Work is the most sophisticated exercise or practice in the world because you get paid for it. I call hunger a form of pain. I call loneliness a form of pain. I call "the ol' nothing to do feeling" intellectual hunger. Hunger feelings range from discomfort through agony.

I don't ever allow my students to complain about their life or work. "Cosmic habit force'" is really terrific. Always respond to "How are you?" with positive superlatives when you are in the outside world. The amenities of life have nothing to do with lying. It is good to always be cheerful in public. Hubert Humphrey and John Wayne faced their deaths this way. It inspired many millions of us to wish them well in the next world. Confidence and cheerfulness is always "never a lazy feeling" emotion. They are work feelings. Perfection is no accident. Happiness and cheerfulness are by products of work feelings.

Workaholicism is definitely the best medicine for manic-depression. Depression and paranoia are both classical symptoms of negative feedback activity in our lives. Depression is a form of fear. It is painful. Depression can make us mend our ways like nothing else can. None of us would be alive today if it were not for our pain and depression circuits.
Paranoia is sometimes a form of "worrying in advance." Unnecessary paranoia is a serious neurosis. Poverty paranoia is definitely connected with manic depression syndromes. Let us face it, fear is part of reality. It is here to stay. Understanding is the why and wherefore of fear and is a super useful part of our education.

A completely fearless person is not a completely educated person. Don't be afraid of being afraid. It is part of the range of human emotion. Anyone in their right mind is capable of feeling fearfulness. The sometimes aspect is what makes it normal.

Unnecessary fear can cause imaginary restrictions to stymie our lives. All of us can be afraid or not afraid of the same thing for similar of different reasons. It is always related to our previous experiences. Dr. Joyce Brothers of America once said the following interesting words, to wit, "There is nothing wrong with paranoia if you don't take it seriously."

Panic is an amplified or overdosed fear reaction.

That means whether it is real or imaginary. It freezes our logical action circuits. Paranoia can sharpen our survival razor of skill. This only happens when it is felt in its proper perspective. Paranoia, like repetition, dulls the human emotions.

Remember: "Guts" makes us accept adversity and challenges. Anything gets smaller the instant you accept it. The opposite of accepting the need to fight adversity is called "shunting." Shunting necessarily magnifies anything. This little tid-bit should definitely open new horizons for you in your Karate classes.

Don't Forget: "Guts = the proper utilization of natural fear feelings. Fear and education are related the same way guts and implicit action are."

Having a just cause is part of the guts superiority part. There is no person in the world who does not like to feel personally safe and secure with his or her well being at all times. The shotgun over the mantle-piece is a good sign that the owner of the home is aware of the need for an adequate self defense mechanism to protect life and property with.

Don't Forget: "Enough" pain is a religious experience. Even presidents and kings must go to school to learn "how to smile real good."

UNEDUCATED PEOPLE
DO NOT FEEL UNEDUCATED.

Sometimes in inaction there is action. When in doubt or panic, it is better to do nothing and do. "Yes" is a positive answer or response. "No" is a negative answer or response. "No answer" is an answer! Sometimes it is the loudest of all. I teach my students to look around, check it out, think ahead, decide, and then do implicitly! Avoid getting hurt or killed, do something useful and above all, finish! That is the "kata" for confronting a fearsome new unknown.

A truly polished self-defense mechanism includes for the ability to ignore an insult. It is best not to react to what you do not relate to. Politicians all know that a person is as big as the small things that can bother him or her. "Yawning at an insult" is a slick way of responding to an indignity with dignity. Spitting at an insult is an aggressive instance of reacting.

Nothing beats a "punch in the face" when there is nothing else appropriate. "No reaction" is sometimes the most clever reaction. Shunting is sometimes called "an apparent no reaction reaction." There are times when shunting is part of good manners. Everyone shunts when anyone passes air in church or in an elevator.

Everyone in their right mind does not forget insults. Serious personalities do not take insults or threats lightly. It is always best to consider the source.

Most Karateists respond to verbal insults with stone cold direct physical violence. It often depends on their particular personality. I teach that an insult is really only yours, "if or when" you accept it, otherwise, "it is still the property of the person who cast it." The Chinese, as well as the Japanese, believe that "nothing can shock a good Karate person."

Most good fighters forgive and forget, "but first get even in triplicate." Great Dane dogs do not hold grudges. People and cats do. Bodyguards, lawyers, dogs and guns are used all over the world as tried and true extensions to a workable self-defense mechanism.

"The cowardice alternative" is a relatively rigid and rigid mode of behavior which is unacceptable male behavior in all societies. It is primarily the fear of getting hurt, damaged or killed that triggers off this type of self-defensive behavior. Cowering, ducking, crying and trembling, covering up the face, stomach and genitals, is practiced by people and animals. I have not yet studied the self-defense mechanisms of plants and insects enough to know. I suspect that it does have its equivalent.

In these modern days, it is equally unacceptable female behavior. The cowardice reaction prevents action which might lead to undue clarity, change or pleasure on a constricted individual's part. This is because it might be incompatible with the continuing neurosis.

Neurotic constriction is probably life saving at the time of its initiation. It generally agreed that a very young and physically immature organism has not had time to be taught or develop its self-defense mechanism. (The ability to support themselves.) The goal of all parents is to get their offspring to that point in life. Sometimes it takes over thirty years with the human species. An adult organism (parents) faced with a similar environmental emergency for the first time, "might solve the emergency by choice." There are far too many variables for behavioral constants to be accurately predicted. My horoscope followers disagree.

There is such a thing as instinctual fear. (Baby gorillas born in captivity, tremble at the sound of drums.) Instinctual fear is not imaginary. There is always a reason for the reaction in nature's design of anything self-defense mechanism.

I make my young black belt teachers remember the golden rule of teaching and that is: "No matter how difficult it is to do, the needs of the group must always determine the day's training program." Students must always depart the dojo knowing more than when they came in. Students must never see a professional teacher or therapist of any type exhibiting less than a super normal attitude and excellence in the performance of the Sensei job. It is easier to excuse even one's own surgeon of error than it is to commit errors as a Sensei of Karate.

Proper professionals help people as well as lead people. Help is leadership. They do this by example all the time and never by mandate. That is why Zen is such a respected discipline and religion throughout the entire world, no matter where you may go. No one hates Zen people. That is because begging is a sin in Zen.

A good shepherd builds seekers and "not followers." A Zen trained teacher or leader does not want followers of any kind. Seekers are superior and won't cost you money. They belong in shepherd's school.

Followers are found in cults and not in dojos of the classical martial arts variety. Follower will cost you money and or your life. Don't even make the members of your family followers of your will. Make them seekers of wisdom and truth.

The professional teacher makes a living by selling his or her knowledge, time and human work energies to the pupils. To do this for life, you must write many books. There is no other way. The Chinese have taught us as teachers, "They who master the pen =

(I.B.M. today), shall never carry the begging bowl."

I must further confess in these Karate confessions, that Zen psychotherapy is another term I coined in the Westernization and Americanization of the Goju Karate discipline. I brought a good thing back with me from Japan, where I spent my young student days working for the United States Navy and the Department of the Army.

Because of these jobs, I had the very good fortune to live and work there for many years to finish my Karate education. I feel that I have had the three greatest teachers and professors in the world. I recognized them as such at that time and memorized everything I could learn.

I essentially was at the right place at the right time in history and knew it. That was the biggest bit of luck in my life. The rest is all working without benefit of luck. I just had one main kata in life, to wit, I enjoy planning my work and then working my plan.
The great sword teachers of Japan's martial arts history were really Zen psychotherapists of the most sophisticated variety. Our TV Kung-Fu stories ala Carradine, Lee, etc., definitely show that quite clearly. Just follow the story line and get inspired by only the "Zatoichi" movies series of Japan. Shintaro Katsu is the most sophisticated artist in history.

Whenever my students complained or questioned anything in our training sessions together, I oftentimes invoked my favorite saying, to wit, "It is part of your training!" Those students who later became teachers, now say the same thing to their students.

The word "sometimes" is the most often used sound in my Zen sayings. I teach my students that the sound of one hand clapping is a good Karate slap in the face of a stupid student, who shunts! Shunting makes marksmanship impossible and courage unnecessary. Remember those words all your life!

There is no adequate self-defense mechanism for any individual thing or society of things, that does not include for the ability to inflict "severe hurtfulness." In time of war, doctors and medical personnel, as well as translators and cooks, are not as readily killed by their captors as those with "killing training." Doctors and cooks have implicit needfulness by the very virtue of their job skills. It is a great self-defense mechanism at any time.

Diplomatic immunity is another marvelous thing for anyone to have. It is also interesting to note that in an elevator with an assassin, it is far better to have had a "splendid Karate education." All professional body-guards know that without their profession, political civilization as we know it today, and throughout history, could never exist.

I teach all my students that it is expensive not to practice. It costs money not to practice enough. Time is money, both the teacher's time and the student's time. I teach the young students who are learning how to manage themselves and their lives, "to never shunt money." Going after your money (marks and grades in school) is part of earning it. Never leave money or money talk as an unresolved issue in any conversation or anything else in human communications. People used to shunt sex talk in the old days. It is now impolite to shunt money talk.

The tournament experience should be part of every Karate Sensei's work for the benefit of the students. Professionals know that pressure builds diamonds. Tournaments build pressure. Teachers engineer the tournaments. The competitive experience, with the fight experience, in tournaments, is feared the most by students with an inaccurate superiority complex.
The favorite pastime of the young second and third dans in any good American Goju dojo is always jiu-kumite (fighting practice). It is the name of the game in any classical Karate dojo.

Senseis deal with people building. They use "human engineering" outlooks in the performance of their job. Children of Karate parents are fortunate. They will invariably learn how to fight real good at a much earlier age than others.

It is important for parents to see to it that their youngsters are provided with a proper understanding of the need to know about violence in the real world. Never allow children to see Karate training as a game. It could ruin them for life in the real world when they grow to adolescence.

Remember: Most people shunt the psychological term "defense mechanism" when it pops up in conversation, or when you volunteer it. Most youngsters think that it is something sinful like the word masturbation used to be the old days. People even shunt the word God in conversation and sometimes in churches.

Shunted things are not normally volunteered. Most people don't talk about how much money they make or what their religion is. This is because that information could be ammunition in the hands of an enemy or a friend. This applies to even a spouse or a brother or sister or colleague, or anything. It is a good social defense mechanism and quite normal everywhere.

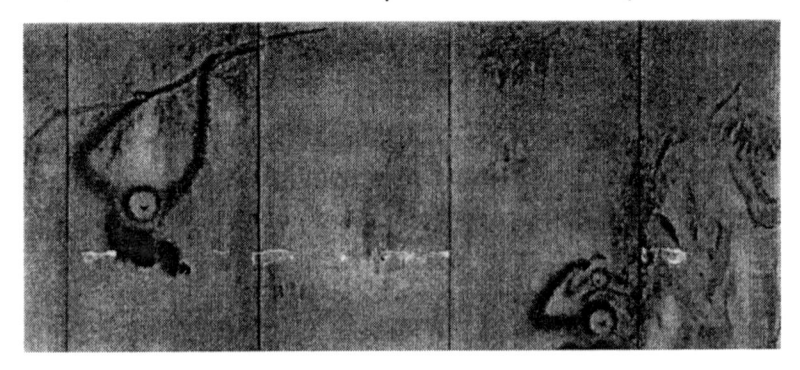

EDUCATION IS ONE BIG COMPETITION.

I confess that I see chess playing as an utterly marvelous therapy. It has a lot in common with fighting practice. Freud was once overheard to have said, "The first thirteen years of orthodox therapy with rich patients is usually bullshit." I would be inclined to believe that. It is good business with most therapy and or disciplines to take a long time in the business of getting down to business. Chess therapy does not allow for that!

I teach my students that one is as good as one's last game. The only game in the world that counts is "the one that one is playing at the moment." The greatest game one ever played in one's life is always "the next game." There is nothing else!

The most often used word, common to a machine gunner, a chess player, a whore, a brain surgeon, an immigration officer and a good fighter is : "Next!" My students learn that in chess, kata, weapons and jiu-kumite, "If practice makes perfect, what the hell do you think perfect practice does?" I use signs like that over the punching bags in my dojo.
I like using symbols like "the square root of infinity" as a code term denoting the meaning of effort. I copied it from my favorite female teacher. Senseis

use every means they can to encourage development of the work ethic. Imaginative and spiry words are the best tools of the trade. I tell students: "Work makes you free, but over time makes you rich." They eventually all accept that as reality.

I humorously cajole them into considering "workaholicism" as a "superior neurosis." I call alcoholism "demon-rum." Prayer sustains the same relationship to one's homeostasis (life feelings) that exercise sustains to excellence. When prayer becomes a neurosis, it is taken to mean "an excuse for laziness." A classical student and Sensei relationship is therapy of the highest order. Humor and the very choice of words themselves, are excellent tools in the psychological operation.

Remember:
Rest and relaxation are part of work.
Practice capacitates confidence feelings.
Saving money capacitates economic "hit power."
Exercise can be used to capacitate energy reserves.
Mastering patience is mastering capacitation, is mastering the self. Karate training opens our minds to such things.

Remember: Willpower and discipline, are forms of artificial enthusiasm.

Everything else is probably relative.

ZEN IS ZEAL, ENERGY & NOWNESS.

Begin each day as if it were your first.
End each day as if it were your last.
Belief in a future potential is the essence of today.

KEEP PUNCHING!

COMPETITIVE WORK IS HIGHLY PAID.

Falling in love with (patients, or students, or clients, or customers, or whatever you want to call it) is simply plain ol' "Bad Business." The rules of work are simple in any office, to wit, "anything that does not compliment the life of the boss, must of necessity stifle it." This is because people who marry their business, only need a one throne empire. Their lifestyle is "their money making machine." I like those kinds of people. They always have time to talk to you when amateurs won't. That is why many of us like our old doctors better than our young doctors. This goes double for nurses and therapists.

It is far superior to love the art and not the artists. Medicine is superior to doctors. Music is superior to musicians. Karate is superior to Karateists. Therapy is greater than therapists. Love is greater than lovers.

The part of a thing can never be greater than the whole of the thing. Good geometry is always a good guideline in all human relationships. No living thing is greater than life itself. No God is greater than religion itself. Never allow a student to become a patient!! That is the secret of really good Karate therapy. They will try to make you do the work of a therapist in order for them to get out of the work of being a good Karate student. Socializing is "not part of their training." Punching bags, sweating and fighting and memorizing new knowledge are! Never work for free and "never take free money." Both of them should not exist.

Many Karate teachers have observed that girls in general feel embarrassment, with inhibitions rather like homosexual feelings, when male teachers direct them towards experiencing each other in the actual fighting practice. I personally make everyone practice fighting with all the others in every single class. This is true even for their first lesson that day or night. Any other system is shunting.

The name of the game in any dojo is always jui-kumite. Always make a first day student get that impression on the first day.
Young teachers will come to observe that girls feel about fighting other girls the way boys feel about dancing with other boys. Girls prefer to do their practice fighting against males. Boys traditionally like fighting because they are encouraged to do so from youth. I hope it stays that way. Girls can fight as good as boys or better than boys, "only if they want to." It is more difficult to get girls to want to fight really well than it is to get boys to excel against each other.

It is not uncommon for some girls to think that girls are not raped, mugged and even killed by other females in the real world. The "femi-po" mentality identifies this type of thinking. There is no discrimination in the world of reality on these matters ever. Don't forget that!

My now famous x-rated saying, to wit: "A girl's first sexual intercourse is to her as monumental an experience as a boy's first fight" is commonly quoted nowadays. Both experiences are full of imaginary restrictions and fantasy, before and after the fact.

In the confessions I have heard, I have found that most women believe that males value their sex equipment more than their punch power. This is not true! I also believe that girls do not value their mystique power (CW-ism and or large breasts), more than their hit power. "Tit power" is psychological hit power, but nothing beats the confidence of knowing you know how to fight really good. That is the advantage that people with some Karate school in their background have over others.

Girls value a "nice purse gun" as a birthday present from their fathers more than a diamond engagement ring from their lovers. If you don't believe me, try it! A diamond ring can get you pregnant, but a proper legal purse gun can save your life many times over.

I still say that grandma's old fashioned long hat pin was and is still one of the strongest and practical tactical all around self-defense mechanisms ever devised. An appreciation of the "point" and the "wedge" in physics is utterly fascinating when viewed in a martial arts perspective.

I maintain that the point was the very first scientific weapon every devised by man. Animals already had them on their claws and teeth and tusks. Girls generally fear other females who can beat them us physically for more than they fear violently dominant men.

Girls who grow long beautiful strong perfectly manicured fingernails are not only envied by other girls, but also engender a slight fear because of their "eye-scratching hit power potential." Men are afraid of Karate men's big punching knuckles for the same reasons.

I must confess that I get a kick out of my women's lib students when they tell me that only a slave would cook for a man. They hate me most when I tell them that liberation is all in the mind. "Any woman who refuses to cook for her man, deserves a man who will not fight for her." A girl who can cook really good is as superior as a guy who can go out and work really good and bring money home for the family. It is good that girls are superior in cooking.

WALK WITH THE CHI IN YOUR FEET.

Young men want a super gorgeous wife to the same extent that a young lady wants her husband to have a super gorgeous paycheck. It must be remembered that good luck and good looks and good money usually go hand in hand. If a man marries a women more beautiful than he is intelligent or manly, it will come to no good.

Whenever smart people marry stupid people, everyone goes downhill. A husband is oftentimes viewed as a girl's first serious self-defense mechanism. He is supposed to replace dads and brothers and uncles. I make all of my young students accept psychologically from childhood, that they, and they alone, must be able to take care of themselves really good forever. They don't like to hear the forever part.

I like teaching my students to believe that: "If people don't do things, they don't get done!" I have cured a great many young Karate students over the years of "a basic belief in magic" and "an impudent attitude towards logic." Karate trained students with at least two years of serious study, are on the average about eight years more mature in personality and even character, than others. I believe this is because of the development of an excellently adequate self-defense mechanism, to wit, their Karate abilities.

In the philosophical psycho analysis of all of my students over all my life, I teach them things like: "A two paycheck family is better than a one paycheck family." I encourage all newlyweds to both work hard. Making more money for all, from all, is really working at your marriages. I have saved many young marriages that way.

Men must protect! Women must cook! Lousy food has ruined more marriages than mere adultery or lousy people to start with. No meal is complete until the dishes are done! Don't ever let anyone forget that in your family! They will love you more for it. Everyone in the world shunts dishes. Don't blush, cringe of feel unique. You are in good company. That is why restaurants are in business. People all over the world go to them more for "not having to do the dishes," than for the superb cuisine. I do teach my super macho men to help a lot with the dishes and the shopping.

People of small stature who are superior fighters see larger people with no "unnatural prejudices." Lightweight men tend to have more overkill in ferocity of attitude, as well as unpredictable and swift motions. Large women with Karate training are not afraid of most men.

It usually takes a long time to learn that proper practice, plus perfect planning, prevents poor performance. I call that string of p's "A good religion."

I usually identify most splendid things that way. The general problem solving process are my favorite pieces of paper. They are superb to tack on the wall of the family "thinking room." The bathroom is often called the "situation room." Baths and showers and shaves, etc., are always accompanied with thinking and sometimes with singing. Think about that the next time you use the bathroom. It is the only place in the world for privacy in most families, large or small.

I believe that enough useful work can solve any problem in life. It works. It is fun responding to the question, "Do you ever lie?" with the word "sometimes." It is superb Zen. When I am overseas, and people ask me, "Are you Italian?" I reply, "Sometimes, it all depends on the music and the food." Many of my students use my material all the time. We all adore the art of Henry Youngman and his quick one liners. It is an excellent self-defense mechanism to have developed.

Remember: Workaholics use their ablution therapy time in the bathroom every morning, in the manner of a religious ritual beginning each new day. The paycheck of a hard worker is sacred. The paycheck of a family person is a lifesaver. The paycheck of a laborer is dignified. The paycheck of a waitress is deserved. Workaholics always have more that one job. Don't forget that, the next time you get poor or are hungry again.

Productivity highs are the greatest! They beat orgasms and orgies and even food, drink and pot. If you get "work is beautiful feelings" every morning, you are definitely a workaholic. Going to the bank for them is a "going to church feeling."

A lot of people go to church, temple, synagogue, or dojo, to enjoy the productivity highs after each attendance. This is a good thing. So, the next time you see old people going to church, don't look strange at them. They are going to get high! Religion gives people spiritual highs. If you are still young, you won't believe that, but as you get older and older, you will see it for yourself.

I get those feelings from Karate tournaments. Coaches and Senseis get satisfaction from seeing their teams and students win. Parents get it from seeing their kids graduate or get married, etc. It takes an awfully long time to become a master workaholic. Only they know when to stop or change.

I confess that I resented the teacher who taught me how to read minds by observing all body languages. Our voices, our tones, our breathing, our facial expressions (or lack of them), our scratching (of any type), our coughing (most especially coughing language), are all part of our "style" (personality and character). I also include the way we walk, our choice of words, the way we drive our cars, our handwriting (graphology), the way we play chess, dance, sing; even the way we shunt or fight back. In other words: the astute observer can literally read minds accurately from all the data.

I have noticed that dogs exhibit objections by shaking, sneezing, or tembling head motions. Student antagonism to learning about "reading people language," changes to gratitude later. This only happens when they come to the same conclusions about body language and vibe language themselves.

The reason young people must learn to control themselves is to keep their true feelings about anything less than an open book for the world to see. There is no privacy or power available to the undisciplined. Most youngsters end up hating the person teaching them that. There is no exception to this.

No one in their right mind likes to have their inferiorities accurately pointed out by others. Only strangers and professionals may do this for us. Children can not stand their partners or siblings doing that job. Parents and school teachers make the best encouragers. Marine drill sergeants are the best discouragers. Only wisdom can teach us that there is nothing in the world as dangerous as an "inaccurate superiority complex."

The next time you run unto a person, who does "crotch scratching" while talking to you, take it as an accurate sign of contempt. People who blow smoke in our faces, definitely consider themselves to be superior. Pointing at you and touching you means that the doer feels in control of you.

People never touch superiors. To prove that, just ask yourself if you ever touch superiors. You will say no. Even if you have no superiors, you will say no. That is why girls immediately red button guys with loose hands. When a girl feels that she is the object of desirability, touching and proximity rights are bargained for. Transactional psychology then ensues.

In all matters of dealing with others always ask yourself who and or what is the object of desirability in this case. Then, properly label that in your mind. Love affairs usually end once one or the other partner accurately determines: "Who dragged whom up from the streets." "Wow, what an interesting scene occurs when both parties have opposite answers, and in the meantime are living together or married, each thinking and feeling the other way."

It must be remembered that two chronic hypo-glyc-cemiacs can not be friends. "Schizophrenic shunts" fly like sparks when both get hungry. Embarrassing alcoholics and lazy hypo-glycemiacs are bad business. Not feeding oneself connotes a basic belief in magic.

This can be harmful if not fatal to the people around us. Many people with difficult or dangerous occupations have lost their lives through the episodic behavior of undiagnosed hypo-glycemic friends, and even family members. All this happens simply because they did not eat breakfast "again that day."

People will not take their car out on the highway with a gas tank reading of empty. They will do almost anything with their human machine registering hungry symptoms. When drugs are taken in-lieu of food, the cemetery gets crowded quicker and quicker by the population.

Non-congenital obesity complexes go hand in hand with gluttony. Chain smoking is a form of gluttony. Shunting is a form of gluttony. Shunting the next moment of reality away is the name of the game. Super normalcy lies in getting pleasure without the necessity for self-destruction. Pleasure should prolong life.

"When in doubt, be useful!" It is a universal truth that useful prisoners are those who cannot be used like a machine or field animal to do unrewarding labor with. Most militarists view themselves and other people more as machines than anything else. The philosopher doesn't.

Most persons of assertive natures find it completely impossible to forgive without first getting even. Make it a practice in life to get everything out in the open. Prevent harbored umbrage from building up Bad feelings and bad thoughts will eventually express themselves someway, someday, one way or another. That is why I never let anything slide. You won't accumulate any fair weather enemies that way, but neither will you get too many foul weather friends. Selectivity of friends and enemies is a superb self-defense mechanism. It is used by all of us in our right minds.

I have seen young men study Karate for years to get the ability to beat up their fathers, or some kid from the school yard. Some of those "kids" have been even in their twenties. I have seen a young lady who poisoned three pimps in her life, take Karate lessons too.

Threats and beatings have gotten more drunken people killed than even impaired driving skills. No one in their right mind takes to threats lightly. Never forget that all your life. Never feed milk to a cobra! It only makes the venom far more deadly. It took the lives of many snake charmers to learn that little tidbit. I believe that the very best self-defense mechanism against drunken drivers and hostile supermarket housewives is not to compete!

TALK WITH THE CHI
IN YOUR FEET.

A good graphologist never competes with cobras. Astrology knowledge is also an excellent weapon to add to your self-defense mechanism. These two subjects help make it possible to know many things about your friends and enemies that they would never tell anyone and probably don't know about themselves.

There will always be more sheep than shepherds. People who hate work prefer being sheep. When the shepherds get sick, the sheep die. Many people rely on only their lawyers as their main self-defense mechanism. They can only defend against the big problems in life. Your basic self, on a physical level, is the most personal behavioral aspect you have. It is the fear of other people that causes the development of learned and instinctual self-defense mechanisms. Artificial ones cause problems.

The entire criminal justice system is society's self-defense mechanism. The law is the self-defense mechanism of people groupings. Contracts are classical examples of people's fear of "the will to fail" in other people. That is why marriage contracts are taken so utterly seriously in society. Shaking hands upon meeting people has its roots in checking out each others vibes first. It is still used to this day.

Cowboys of the old west had to check their guns at the bar. Many had a boot gun or ankle knife anyway.

They obeyed signs. This does not mean that they believed in them too. Graduates of wolf school are generally criminals. Graduates of shepherds' school are generally called cops. A con man is a graduate of wolf school. A soldier is a graduate of shepherd school. A masochist is a graduate of sheep school.

I must confess that my confessions in this book are meant as lessons and not just stories about myself. I am a firm believer in what I call "radio silence." I always teach my students that volunteered information is always a lie. Keeping one's big mouth shut is always better than blabbering. The word confession itself implies something utterly personal.

It is best to teach only useful things that people don't know already. It is best to always confess only common knowledge. Extraordinary knowledge is best written about for all to see. Confessions are best whispered in church in one's innermost soliloquies.

There is no prayer like that said in a cathedral. There is no confession like that shrieked out in a crowded courtroom. Contrary to popular opinion, priests do not enjoy listening to confessions. People are not interested in what they don't care about to begin with. Talk to God directly whenever necessary. There is no better self-defense mechanism for all of us. It is best that way.

I teach my students that everyone can sing. The only thing that we all have to learn is simply "the difference between natural tone and artificial tone." Some of us are born with a natural singing voice. Some of us are not.

Johnny Carson can sing the song called "Just A Rhinestone Cowboy" quite uninhibitedly and a lot of other good songs, but only in his acting tone or artificial singing voice. Artificial means just anything that is not you naturally, that doesn't mean it's not terrific. Jimmy Durante did not have a natural singing voice tone, yet his fans saw him as the greatest singer/actor/pianist/dancer in the world when he was living.

Most everyone has a natural inferiority complex about not being able to sing too good. Don't sing in a natural tone or character if you don't have a natural tone or character to begin with. Always do what you do best, the way you do it best! The one good thing about alcohol is that it and singing go quite hand in hand. Fighting does too. The conclusion is simple, to wit, "inhibitions prevent naturalness." A natural singer is his or her own character.

The next time you are in a singing mood or environment, put it to the test. Ninety percent of the world's money making professional singers are essentially artificial singers. So what! Ninety percent of the world's marriages are artificial. So what! We are all artificial when on stage or tape or camera, or even in print. That is the way it is supposed to be.

Remember: Anyone not capable of being artificial, is not capable of surviving in the real world. If you were a president, could you make an effective speech on TV without it?

Putting on your make-up or shaving in the morning is real artificiality. Naturalness is best seen in the box at a funeral parlor, or in an incubator box in the new arrivals room at any maternity centre. The only things to stay absolutely pure about in our lives is of course logic and math!

Computers can give us artificial intelligence, hospitals can give us artificial parts, school and books can give us artificial minds. The only thing to stay away from is "artificial logic or artificial math."

FIGHT WITH THE CHI IN YOUR HANDS.

I find that a good therapist never lets a student tell him or her too much. That is what is meant by the old saying: "Too much knowledge is a dangerous thing." It seems that most people will tell their Karate teacher, their barber, their accountant, their butcher and their mistress or consort, everything! Most people save the unimportant things for their expensive analyst anyway.

For some unknown reason, most people will tell more truth about themselves in the dentist's office. Surgeons and pastors agree to my findings. Taxi drivers agree with me all the way concerning people shunting in their taxi cabs. Some stupid people blabber on and on out loud in cabs; as if there were really no one listening. (There is the shunting! What the hell do you think the driver is doing?) Cab psychology is the most interesting in the world. It ranks along with elevator psychology.

It is not uncommon in many places for husbands and wives to know nothing important about each other, once the marriage ceremony is over. Most high school teachers know more about the kids than the parents do. Female analysts have told me that the thing they hate most is a female patient who competes with the doctor.

Karate therapists are capable of beating their students up. This factor contributes a lot to the utterly civilized conduct in all Karate schools anywhere in the world. A shock therapist is a Sensei who punches his or her students in the face. This happens when the student gets unduly stupid or utterly uncivilized on purpose.

"The on purpose part" is what makes shock therapy (ala Karate) such a splendid tool of the profession. It often times is the most gentle way to straighten out "the ol' bad thinking."

I once met a lovely therapist who would beat her patients up if they didn't get well or stayed pathological liars all their lives. There is a lot to be said for shock therapists. Sometimes, students who are educated beyond their intelligence, get straightened out by it in one session.

I have had several Reichian analysts, as well as military psychologists, study Karate with me and adopt my therapy methods. Schizophrenics in particular, find the most difficulty in trying to hide their fear of fighting in open group training. Karate therapy systematically evaporates artificial defense mechanisms. It replaces them with stone cold reality thinking.

My friends told me that no publisher would touch my book if I kept my insistence that Karate be spelled with a capital letter. I shall simply publish myself. I want Karate to be a capitalized word because it is a religion to too many of us. I am interested in seeing what happens with me neurotically sticking to this point. Time will tell.

Recluse-ism is the most common self-defense mechanism. It is used a great deal by our fearful elderly and other crime victims. This is especially true in New York City. "Fear of subways" is a sane and sober reality there, but not in Moscow. Many "loners" defend themselves by making their world smaller and smaller. The loner type personalities of the world are usually developed in childhood. It is a behavioral mode that protects. It keeps one from dealing with others in the real world.

A bully is nothing more or less than a sadistic coward. The beautiful words, "They who live by the sword, die by the gun," really mean: "Hit persons get hit." I teach that the best way to fight a weapon is with another weapon. Fight fire with water. Eternal vigilance is always the price of freedom from fear. There is nothing else. It can never be given. It can only be developed by the self. New York City once had a case of an elderly couple actually committing suicide together in their tiny apartment because they were too terrified of going outside. They could not take living in fear anymore. That shows the extent to which the mind will go.

Old parents do not want to live with their children to impose on their sacred privacy. They really want their children to protect them from being killed in their old age. Children who do not protect their aged and helpless parents, are destined to face the same world of terror some day.

An old African saying goes, "To kill the father or mother, one must first of all kill all the sons and daughters." I believe in filialpiety. The elderly are not afraid of dying. They are afraid of being ignominiously killed by most juvenile murderers. The proof of this is that old people are never murdered by other oldsters.

Capital punishment is more conducive to capital safety than the nonsense of not paying for life with life. It is best to kill killers. Primitive cultures do not feed and shelter killers. Only advanced ones do. The question arises, "Advanced in what?"
There is a proper time and place for everything under the sun. This includes for shock therapy and implicit social action. The lack of implicit law definitely fosters mass-neurosis. Vagrants see everyday life as just one moment to moment horror adventure in super paranoia. Paranoia goes hand in hand with alcoholism and drug addiction.

In the real world, fish eat fish. It is the fear of being sodomized or killed by other prisoners that keeps youth on the up and up in the outside world. Guards do not "practice" brutality as our movies have us believe. They are just as scared as the prisoners.

Spirit, talent, and genius are related to instinct. Genius is knowing how to do things you were never taught. Karate psychology teaches us to protect our spirits as well as our bodies. Swiftness comes only from effort. Religion is the self-defense mechanism of our spirits. Spirit (soul) is the only thing we came into this life with and it is the only thing we go out with. I don't believe we can take our educations. Time will tell on that one.

The spirit uses the mind to operate our machines (bodies). The spirit is the driver, the body is the car. When the driver leaves the car, by choice or by accident, the car is no longer alive (animated). I do not know what happens to, or with the spirit then, but I'm rather sure it's a continuum of some sort. I think we get a new machine in the next world.

Mental health is the art of "organizing the self" and good house cleaning. Improvement of our spirit's equipment is the name of that game. I find that a structured time existence, in conjunction with a structured environment, make for the best mental health for me. Knowledge, laughter and food, as well as love and friendship, are the best medicines for the entire entity called "us." It is the duty of all of us to be able to take care of ourselves. This is called Urban's law.

Serenity comes from old knowledge. Progress comes from new knowledge. Our collective historical universal subconscious may well still be in the embryo stage or earlier. My guess is that it is too early to tell yet. The voice of the inside is the one to guide. Discard everything else. When in doubt, "Do nothing and do!" When flustered, "Stop guessing!"

I have had quite a few students. Some became well known lawyers. They have the strongest mystique of all serving them. Everyone is afraid not to pay lawyers. This is not the case with teachers, doctors and dentists. People resent paying money for being made well. They feel that their pain at that time, somehow or another miraculously exempts them from paying other people for getting them well. Do not worry about that. Everyone feels that way about something in life.

All hard working people must keep in mind that, "Anything is more valuable before you get it than it is after you got it." This is called "Urban's second law of reality." Men and women hate to pay whores, electric bills and income taxes. Don't worry about that either. The whole world is that way.

Do not forget: Getting pregnant, "having babies not on purpose" is caused by shunting and if you think about it for a moment, you will nod your head in agreement. Would you want to be born not on purpose? There are no accidents in sex. Both people must be in control of themselves forever. Shunting is stupid.

I confess that I am one of the many Senseis of America who were teaching martial-arts to our youth during the 1950's and '60's. We all have an exquisite pride of accomplishment in our work. It has always gone unheralded until now. Many thousands of young men, who survived the military experience, came home to thank their Karate and Kung-Fu teachers for the priceless gift of the hard training. They thanked their teachers before they even went to see their wives and families.

Karate became a part of their lives in their youth. It then saved their lives in their adulthood. The rigors of military training were not difficult for them. The combat experience was nothing new or shocking. The Senseis knew that would be the case while they were training the kids. The Karate students were the beneficiary generation of something quite useful to them for life.

Many parents have come to realize, years later, that if it were not for the Karate teachers, many of their kids would be gonners today. This applied to the drug scourge as well. Drug addicts were the only kids who couldn't make it in those days. All the graduates made something of themselves in life because of Karate school. Lazy adults weren't even able to survive a day in the dojos of that era.

I enjoy using colorful and imaginative language as a psychological ploy. It is best used to impress a point of new knowledge. I would say things like: "Only two people know this and one is dead." They never forget whatever follows that opening statement. I make them accept that it is easier to stay out of trouble than it is to get out of it, once you are in it!

Everyone lies sometimes, but in Karate circles, not only does one get punished for what one lied about, but also for the very act of lying as well.

Anyone who says they have never lied, just did with that statement.

I use a code term called "pushing the red button" to describe the mental process of "dropping one's emotional dedication." The wrong word at the right time can change love or respect to fear or hatred in a split second. I have found that keeping a large red push button with the word "reset" printed on it, makes for an excellent mental health artifact or toy. It does an impressive job.

Everyone who believes in telling it like it is, most of the time, should have a red button on their work table or in their minds. I use mine along with coughing and gagging to expel bad feelings. I press it every time I get a bad idea and realize it as such. I tell my students that a bad idea dropped is better than a good idea done! It is better to do nothing and do, (sometimes), than to undo stupidity. Mistakes cost money. Stupidity and neurosis don't just kill time for us, they murder it.

"Bamboozling" occurs when people deviate from the original premise. I am always on the alert for this, particularly when listening to a speech of persuasion. Really superb discourse is superior to intercourse. In both things, "bamboozling" is a problem causing factor.

It is best to object immediately when your friends and enemies drift from the original premise. Don't let anyone color your book with their verbal-pastel-crayons. "Coloring book jobs" cause more misunderstanding and nonsense games than any other defensive techniques people use in lying to and with each other. Being aware of exactly when people drift from the original premise, either purposefully or otherwise, is an excellent piece of ammunition to put into your self-defense mechanism.

Shunting is a form of bamboozling the self.

When we do this to ourselves by accident, it is called misfortune. When we do this to ourselves on purpose, I call it retarded behavior designed to avoid work feelings of one type or another. Amateurs shunt, pros don't!

When the law does this to us on purpose it is called justice, by accident it is called a mistake. Stone walls do a prison make and iron bars a cage indeed. Religion tries to explain it.

Remember: Anger is a form of capacitated energy. You can imagine why cops and even high level governmental professionals get themselves slashed, cut, stabbed, shot and or killed because they haven't been trained enough in the mastery of the art of recognizing when and how it occurs.

The ability to read human and animal as well as machine capacitation signals in other people (particularly the phenomenon of eye dropping) is a technology of literally predicting their next and every move thereafter in fighting, chess playing and debating. This people language reading ability will keep you from getting hurt in a fight or disillusioned in a lifetime.

It is important to view oneself as living in all three dimensions of reality at the same time. To wit: Firstly and always, in the here and now of course; as well as, in the past and the future. It is all one concomitant reality. No one of these elements can or does exist independently. Think about that and how non-neurotic it is to view them all as equally real and all quite different in size.

We can measure and manipulate the here and now. The past can be partially measured and determined, but never manipulated. The future can not be measured. The past can not be ignored, the present can not be ignored. One has a choice in the here to come. It is fun to work now, read yesterday and plan tomorrow.

I once helped a severe schizophrenic who was infamous for practicing medicine on himself without a license. It told him that he was not crazy. His friends and family believed he was mad. I told him that he was a genius gone mad. I used these words in front of his friends and family. My comment not only saved face for him, but also gave a psychological out to mend his ways.

It wasn't long before he took on the behavior of a "genius gone sane." He subsequently finished his college education and became a thousandaire before the age of thirty. This case quite surprised me. I chalked it off as another excellent memory of the Zen psycho therapeutic approach in the magic of applied psychology. Reverse psychology works much better with adults than it does with children. It must always be camouflaged.

"The silent language" is always taken more seriously than the real thing. This is because the shadow of a thing is always bigger than the thing itself. This is true in anybody's language, body language, vibes language or otherwise.

I confess that I have been prejudiced and stupid most of the time. This lasted until I got my maturity together, (the suparempei mind). Maturity occurs when we know our limitations. I like to define hope as knowing things in advance without confirmation!

I hold that prejudice is a form of "worrying in advance." It is usually about theoretical generalities that are taken to hold true for the whole. Prejudices are also contrived as self-defense mechanisms to avoid disruption of safe neurotic procedures. Prejudice is useful when there is not enough time to be scientific.

The prejudice emotion leads to a termination of total contact or engagement of an inadequately mechanized defense system with the emergency situation upon which it is predicated, or which it denotes. If the emergency situation is not disengaged, the typical neurotic defense tends to disengage with something else. It may not be at all germane to the original premise.

Gradually changing vision causes many people to start hating books and reading. They do this instead of hating their eyes. They start hating things that they are supposed to see well. This analogy is very useful to people who keep diaries and enjoy self-analysis. Sometimes some people make their vision go bad in order to have a good excuse to keep from reading anything. Karate teachers generally hold that only one out of every five people do not predicate their self-defense mechanisms on a subconscious pathology that is not rooted in fantasy.

I have learned from my own teachers that rage, fear, pain, grief, sadness and withdrawal, constitute emergency emotions. By their particular quality, they imply the mode (modality) of their most expeditious termination. Harbored-umbrage (bad vibes) is especially to be avoided. It can cause cancer and early death in men and women. Never hold on to harbored-umbrage. It will eventually always manifest itself in one way or another. Only time can erode it completely. Expression is best. Immediately is preferred. You can get rid of bad feelings mechanically using my gagging procedure.

It is sometimes true in life that the only way to get rid of a temptation feeling is to give in to it. "Get it off your chest" actually means that. Feelings actually manifest themselves in your machine (body). The tight chest, painful neck, and bad back syndromes, are perfect examples of this. Mental health is the equivalent of driver education for your machine. Prayer is really sophisticated mental health.

Harbored-umbrage is also weighty. Fighters feel great after punching the hell out of the heavy bag and then each other. They don't generally know the psychological why and wherefore of such therapeutic activity, but they are aware of the feelings. Nature sometimes makes the bodies of people and animals vomit to release bad feelings, as well as poisonous substances from the stomach. Poisonous feelings must be expelled before they do their work internally.

A lot of the kids who saw the "Rocky" movie ask questions in the gyms and dojos around the world. The answer to all of them is very simple. No! Orgasms before the fight are poisonous to your killer spirit if you have one to begin with! Fighters who care more about their tension control than about "the bout" deserve to be on their backs more than on their feet. No youngsters (boys and girls) believe that. They change their minds if they are able to stick in the game.

People who know they can fight real good are immediately sensed to that way by others. Confidence vibrations are easily discernable as fear vibrations are. Do not forget the "as easily part." It is for this reason that the heavy-weight champion of the world is the "symbolic king of men." Muhammid Ali affected minds and history books forever.

Black people throughout the world take more pride in that, than even being a pope or a president. It is interesting to note that all non-black peoples of the world feel exactly the same way for exactly the same reasons.

Even the elderly wealthy value physical security feelings more than opulence securities. The late Howard Hughes of America is an example that makes me think of that. Bob Hope of America is the "symbolic king of mental health." Many of our successful elderly use him as their role image Johnny Carson is "the symbolic king of TV performers."

I have seen that both pleasure and significant or remarkable creativity, require as a necessary condition, total contact or engagement of the living organism with the situation in which such feelings are experienced. It must be remembered that not all pleasures are not harmful or injurious over the time of contact. Gluttony is a perfect example of this.

Compulsive chain smoking is the most common of all human pleasures. I have a theory that people who have been smoking all their lives must of necessity continue; to achieve their maximum longevity. I know this is shocking and probably never propounded by doctors before, but I have seen people who started smoking at six years old and are still on television at ninety-six years old. Eubie Blake is a classical example. Quitting smoking when it's too late can put the elderly into an earlier grave.

The old Italian ladies overseas used to tell me that too much wine makes one stupid. Too much sleep makes one tired, weak, sick and can even cause death. Too much sex causes weakness and laziness. Too little sex causes nervousness and shunting. Too little sleep always causes illness and disorientation. Sleep is the most precious medicine we have.

Sleep must be used as a daily medicine and not as an illicit narcotic. Don't ever turn it into a form of coffin practice. None of us ever have to practice for that. Alcoholics and the severely depressed are the most susceptible to over-dosing on sleep. Some creative writers and inventors know how to use sleep time to do problem solving with.

I once asked a root canal specialist what the highest high in the world was. She said, "Why you damn fool, the relief of pain is of course," Migraine sufferers agreed. Arthritics know that all their lives.

I know of many people who get educated beyond their intelligence and still run into despair feelings in their forties. There is no such thing in this world as a person who has never prayed. I always tell my students to do the best with what they've got and do it now. Talking to yourself is a form of praying. Planning things is a form of prayer. Prayer is the only thing to do when there is nothing else.

Reaction, in lieu of action, is triggered off by fear of embarrassment feelings. I also call this the neurotic shunt. The inability to deal with such real feelings causes the mind to pretend that "nothing ever happened, or is not happening right now, or will it really happen." The pathological subconscious literally shunts off truth messages. This happens when we are caught in telling lies. Pain is the only medicine for this. Humor and or shunting off reality messages as a reaction to death is not necessarily shunting. It is a form of respect and culturally correct behavior at Irish funerals and wakes. This brings up the question, "Why do people sometimes cry at weddings?"

Laughter is not uncommon in disaster situations. It is one of our human ways of using shunting to deal with stark reality situations. It is sometimes the only self-defense mechanism available in lieu of a socially unacceptable panic reaction. It must be remembered that "shunting is pretending." Hysteria is magnification. Neurosis is any consistency ....

sometimes!

I know very much that "repetition dulls the emotions." I teach this to all my students; especially the lazy ones. It is the best tool we have, however, for sharpening our razor of skill and memorizing things.

Our pathological subconscious is our collection of neurotic shunts of a subconscious nature. They correspond to a defect in the ability to concentrate for very long repetitive processes. That is why I am fond of making my students learn things while I keep them in motion. Sometimes they are kept in a state of pain as a captive audience.

I do not go for static learning. I allow kids to do their homework with the radio or TV on. There is such a thing as divided concentration for certain tasks. "The right music" and news can get an awful lot of work done. Even the meanest sweat shops know this little secret. Silence is like darkness to groups of people. It slows things down.

Music and sound in public buildings and transportation facilities, cuts down on crime and paranoia feelings by keeping people from picking up on or zeroing in on each other's vibes. Even animals like it sometimes. Music is a tremendous self-defense mechanism. People generally whistle when they are experiencing inner happiness feelings as well as fear feelings. That is quite interesting about us. We do not pray when we are joyous. People pray when they are fearful or depressed.

I consider prayer to be the quintessence of magic. Prayer does a lot of things to people and for people that music does. Hypnotism it seems, is at the centre of it. People practice more auto hypnosis than we know. Knowledge itself is magic. My favorite Karate saying is: "They who are afraid of life, do not know Karate." "They who are afraid of death do not have a religion."

Remember: Practice capacitates confidence feelings. Saving money capacitates economic "hit power." Exercise can be used to capacitate energy reserves. Mastering patience is mastering capacitation, is mastering the self. Karate training opens our minds to such things.

THINK WITH THE CHI
IN YOUR MIND.

I best define the non-pathological subconscious as implicit behavior. The ideal self-defense mechanisms in Karate address themselves to the implicit. The "grandma BB system" is slang for beatings and bribery. Most of us have been raised that way or are raising others that way. It works better in training animals than raising people

Robotized dogs are trained that way exclusively. I prefer my dog to be territorially motivated by love. There is no self-defense mechanism as marvellous as a dog that has adopted you. Remember, we do not adopt them, they psychologically adopt us or they don't. Love can not be beaten into or out of anything.

I make it a practice to promote my new students to the green belt level of Karate skill only when they exhibit increasing initiative, drive and appear to have more inside development directions. Of all the belts in the world, green belt is the most difficult to achieve. Some students can make it in only six months; some students take six years. Therein lies a good case for my "bubonic laziness theory."

I use a slang phrase, "The high executioner for the ASPCA." It describes a syndrome. It concerns people who's jobs keep them in reality feelings all the time. Police, judges, referees and umpires especially; along with surgeons, ambulance drivers and firemen, develop an inability to not be able to feel life for themselves. Many of them keep their "perpetual responsibility feelings" in the on position, even when they are not on the job. There are many professions in the world like that. Some people are only capable of relaxing if they are on the job working. Working does relax people. They have to honestly love and enjoy their work, however, for that to be the case.

It seems that the more serious the job in the real world, the less and less one scores on "the social applause scale." No one ever applauds a beautiful burial ceremony. They do hold the priest responsible for everything however. Always pay the priests of your religion. It is not a sin to compliment a priest for a beautiful wedding ceremony. Very few people thank the priests for listening to their confessions. Bartenders get tipped real money for doing the same thing priests and other professionals do for free. The more serious the job in the real world, the less the pay. Firemen not only don't get tipped or applauded socially, they usually get criticized unless enough of them died trying to do the impossible.

I tell my students, who have dropped out of school, that they have either "the bubonic laziness" or "the bubonic superiority feelings." People don't feel what you feel about yourself. People don't even see what you see in the mirror. Unfriendly people don't feel that way about themselves. They think that their main problem is being too good to the world. This is not an uncommon disease in show business and professional athletics.

People appreciate small things being pointed out for them. No one in the world likes the big things pointed out for them, however. don't forget that. It's an important point in understanding how to live with others in this world.

I call spontaneous remission "changing one's mind" or "talking the self out of a bad idea." When some of my students get overbearingly erudite with me in our conversations, I always tell them that I have heard more words that I have read. Teachers and students have one thing in common, they never like to be talked down to or shot over.

Karate people are so respected because they can fight real good with and without weapons. Most of the world's people can only fight real good with weapons. Shunters hate Karate schools for that reason.

Too much fantasy fighting practice can permanently retard a student's ability to contact reality. The word shunting itself, implies a let's pretend mentality. Simulation is profiting from experience in advance, but shunting is an emotional thing. I tell my students who want to be Karate Senseis, that their livelihood will depend upon retailing a discipline. Discipline is the one thing in the world that most people spend their entire lives and fortunes avoiding at any cost. Anyone retailing a discipline can never become a millionaire. This is called "Sarah's law."

I have found that there are certain words everyone shunts. For example, one will never hear the word "mutiny" uttered, even in jest, in any military grouping anywhere. The word embezzlement is not even thought about in a finance and accounting office. The words fight and violence, are too real to the unfamiliar or unequipped to be used commonly. They are literally afraid of the real words. The word "con" is used by con-persons in-lieu of the word lie. A liar hates to be lied to more than any other person-in the world. Never forget that little tid-bit. You will find many uses for it throughout life.

Most men do not use the word coward for the same reason that homosexuals do not use the word "Queer." The word corpse, or stiff, is never used in a funeral parlor. It is perfectly alright in a morgue however, provided that one is not speaking to one of its close relatives. Abortionists shunt the word baby in preference to the word fetus.

Lawyers use the word "altercation" in-lieu of the word fetus. Couples use the phrase fooling around or "chipping off" instead of the word adultery.

Television evangelists always shunt the word adultery. Television evangelists always shunt the word "phony." Ministers use the words offerings, tithes and donations in-lieu of the word money. I say call a spade a shovel and get it over with.

Shunting is here to stay. It is part of the human condition. In essence, Karate psychology, as propounded by my view, revolves around the word shunting and its implications. We all do it for different reasons. It is simply a matter of extent and why. Shunting is used a great deal visually to defend against embarrassment. We can shunt sounds and sights as easily as thoughts and words. Embarrassment is a painful feeling. Shunting is anesthesia. Don't forget that. Shunting pain is the best use we have for the process. I am rather sure that animals shunt too.

Alcoholics only use the word alcoholic when they are sober. People who do not have an adequate self-defense mechanism, even shunt real dangers and real paranoia. The slang for this is "accident-prone." You can only prevent yourself from shunting once you are capable of identifying it. Just the knowledge of the word will save us all millions of mistakes.

It is important for young students to know that alcohol and drugs have played a tremendous part, more than we could ever know, in the history of all combat in all times. Drugged up fighters, like souped up hot rods and souped up race horses, definitely have the advantage in a fight to the death.

I like to designate the words, "war stories" as the therapeutic slang for "exaggeration without the intent to deceive." War stories are taken to mean hyperbole or imaginary deeds of bravery or acts of incredible super normalcy. "Man from La Mancha" is a perfect example. "Quixotic" is the idea.

Such stories vary inversely in interest and intensity according to the innocence level of the listeners. In most cases they are never the same twice. No one in their right mind ever tells really serious stories. Braggarts use war stories in between drinks. It is usually a self-defense mechanism protecting their favorite inadequacy.

Most interesting war stories are told by the young white belts. This is because they don't practice enough. I tell the kids always trying to impress girls, that whatever is not self-evident, "is not evident!" The most impressive thing a person can do is impress themselves. That is not easy to do without shunting some kind of a truth in the process. The need to impress people all the time is an unworthy CW self-defense mechanism. It is uncivilized to the same extent that self-praise is.

I confess that the following famous people were alumni of mine in their student days as Karate enthusiast: No, on second thought, it is far better for me to wait for their memoirs to come out, to see what effect my Karate training had on their lives. Let's see what happens. It could be the foundation of another book for me on them.

I confess that the Japanese tradition of "Senseis never advertise" stuck with me. It is probably neurotic, but, I take great pride in believing that a good Sensei would never advertise. I personally would not utilize a psychiatrist or surgeon advertising openly for his or her business. It is a prejudice of mine that I like. I think it has made more money for me in the long run that the other way. It is also an excellent self-defense mechanism for keeping away the undedicated. Dedication is viewed a lot by some as also a neurosis in an individual. It is viewed as necessary in groups. If it weren't for dedication no one would ever find a cure for cancer and arthritis.

Karate training that becomes a way of life is really for the few, and not the many. It couldn't exist any other way. If the rocky road to mastery were not that way in all arts and sciences, then brothers and sisters, we would all be Ph. D people today. Imagine, if everyone were doctors, who would do the work?

Any Karate style, any organization, can have only one

historic founder in any one country for all time. A founder is the tenth dan executive title for that position. It lasts forever. An elected president takes the place of a dead founder as the living leader of the style or (school of thought). George Washington was a founder. He did not have a previous administration to blame things on. A founder, a discoverer, an inventor, all have that exclusivity.

Presidents can only improve things. That is what they are expected to do. Settlers can only civilize things. Exploiters can only explore and map. There are some things in life, as well as in time, that can not be done twice. That is why I am proud of myself for making American Goju Karate good enough to represent us in the Karate world and in time. I personally feel sorry for any country in the world that has no Karate. A country without Karate will definitely not survive all its wars. The world belongs to those who are in position to accept its responsibilities.

The grand masters of the "college of Kyoshis" (senior masters) vote to make a president. Presidents replace presidents by votes; not for life. That is why the ninth dan of any organization also wears a red belt. It symbolizes the vice presidential job slot. Some oriental martial-arts families and or systems, have taken as long as fifty years after the death of a founder to decide upon who should carry on the work of leadership in the organization.

"Miyagi Chojun" was the founder of the Goju style in the country of Japan. As such, he was also its first tenth dan, to wit, "the wearer of the red belt." There are now, in modern days, some styles, who for one reason or another, use the solid red belt for the identification of low ranks. Only Japan, America, Okinawan Karate systems do not. Remember that if you are a Karate person in the game for life.

Miyagi Chojun designated Gogen Yamaguchi in his will to take the reins of leadership upon Miyagi's death. A tenth dan position inherited from a dead founder, stays the tenth dan for life. Presidents get elected every four years. In the event they don't get re-elected, they keep their red belt and tenth dan rank for all their lives anyway. They are then awarded the title of "tenth dan emeritus" by the American College of dans. This is quite a thing. It is almost as good as being a former mayor of New York City in regards to prestige.

Remember: It is good to make a will. I consider it sound, sober, matured, non-neurotic behavior. Not making a will out means that you think that you are beyond super normal. Well, you know what that means. No will means that you do not care now. When you die, it will be proof to everyone that you never cared in the first place. Even hundredairs. Former thousandaires and multi-thousandaires make perfect plans and wills before they're forty-five years old.

In the old days, a founder was replaced by his eldest blood-son. Such a son was always expected to be made to follow in the footsteps of his father. This is not uncommon in the Orient even today. Westerners don't generally expect the children to follow the path of the father.

There have been literally thousands of great masters who were also founders of family named styles. The dan rank procedure holds true throughout the globe, especially with founders of religious, ministries, arts corporations, and in some cases even politics.

The tenth dan can be compared to the "point rider" position in any organization. The definition of a leader in Karate thinking is: "Anyone who does anything first." "The first part" is the essence of leadership in a nutshell. Holding the line as a tenth dan is only difficult during the first ten years of getting incorporated and published. Your enemies stop firing after that, because they run out of ammunition by then.

A tenth dan is always subordinate to his living teachers. He or she has no rank of superiority, other than student, in the parent teacher's eyes. This feels like you would if your son or daughter became a president or a leader of a country, or something of the status.

I confess that the most difficult thing I had to do in the last twenty years was to further the development of American Goju system in Italia. I had one hell of a time trying to convince the various Karate and Jiu-Jitsu masters there that inter style competition was the only way to have real competition. I showed them that in a one style, one organization tournament, it is a case of "brother against brother."

I had to show the Italian masters that what they were doing was very interesting, but not important! Style against style is important! My Karate work in Italy earned me the social nickname in Padova city of: "Giuseppi Garabaldi." He was the George Washing of Italy, who united the various states and made one country. I found the people to be very much like the Japanese in their social nature. Italy is the place for you if you like adventure.

Italy is no place for people who do not traditionally love hard work seven days a week, forever. It is a workaholic's paradise. The favorite form of suicide there is "to work yourself to death." Alcoholism runs a close second, and politics runs third. Politics overseas is more important to the masses than even religion and art. If you are not interested in politics, you would find all of Europe to be quite dull for conversation and news interests.

I believe that workaholic-ism is really a self-defense mechanism of the rich and famous. It is used to keep them out of trouble and is a superb way to keep from "spending money." When there is nothing to do, workaholics literally sit down and "invent new work!" The very act of "making money" gives them a tremendous high. Waitresses get addicted to receiving tip money every few minutes. In enough hours, days, months or years, the addiction stays forever.

Workaholics do have more fun. Anyone who has experienced "Work is beautiful feelings" is a workaholic. They stay busy all the time. It is the only way in world to stay a together thousandaire. Lazy thousandairs soon become hundredairs again.

I confess that I believe that no one's confessions ever end. I tell my students in my lectures and letters to them, "Never date yourself!" Prepare for old age in your middle age. This is best done by living in first and writing about it only in the past tense. Keep a diary. It is your best analyst. Your diary is your bible. Don't forget that.

Anyone who lies to their diary is crazy or about to go crazy at any given moment. A book that you deliberately lie to is not a diary. They are usually called expense accounts. Good writers must keep accurate diaries.

LOVE WITH THE CHI
IN YOUR EMOTIONS.

Remember: Self caused poverty is a form of laziness, ergo a form of cowardice. All of us who may be lazy hate to be called that word worse than a liar hates being lied to.

Being lazy is a waiting feeling. Ladies love to wait for things. Some people wait by their mailboxes forever.

Remember: The workaholic rich and the workaholic poor both have essentially the same religion. The difference is in the education.

Don't Forget: The essence of all phobias is "shunting" in one way or another. Time and time again you will see this to be the case without exception. Some people take pride in staying poor all their lives because they think that makes them exceptional in some way or another. Begging in any way is the severest form of prostitution.

PROCRASTINATION IS ANOTHER WORD FOR SHUNTING.

RATIONALIZATION IS SOPHISTICATED SHUNTING.

Remember: Perpetual postponement of getting what you want for yourself (on purpose), so that you won't be disappointed, and or being afraid of success because there wouldn't be anything to do afterwards, can be quite excellently summed-up in the word "shunting."

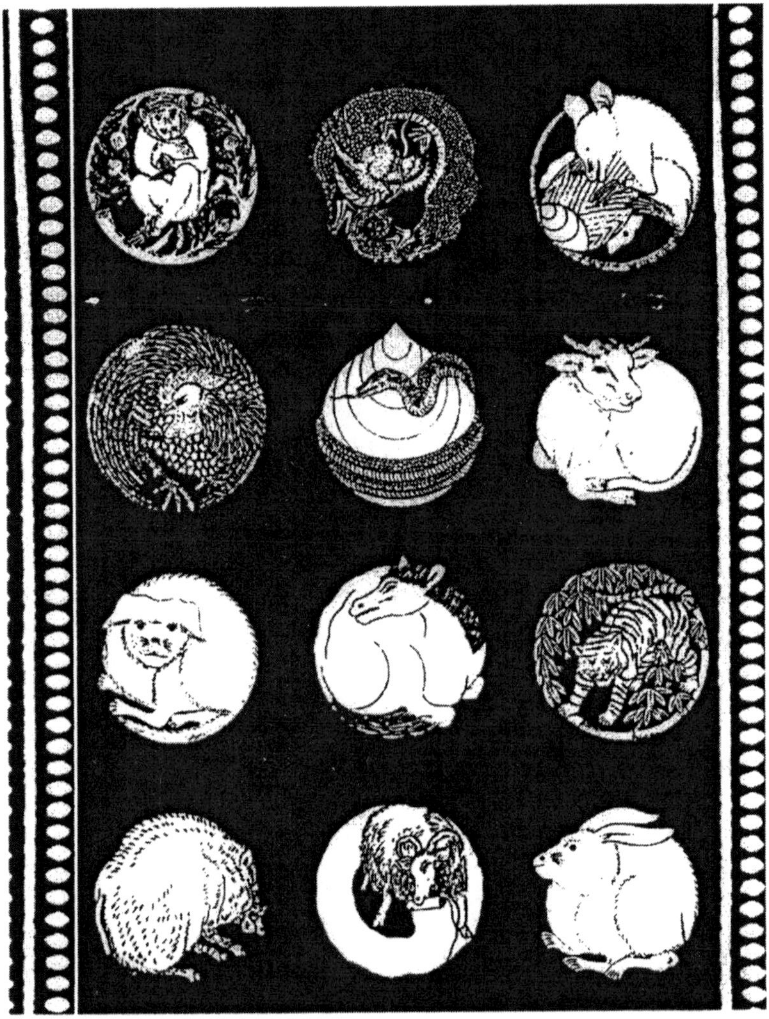

26 CASE HISTORIES

ARNOLD

Arnold's law: The human reliability factor is 15% of what you expect when it comes to loyalty. Only your dog will pass with a 100%.

Arnold was a very famous Karate master in Japan. He could read minds with more fluency that you or I could watch television. He was also an incredible hypnotist. These self defense mechanisms protected his 110 lbs. body from sumo wrestler's, as well as wild animals. He could literally make people or animals feel fear-feelings at his will. Arnold's personal style of fighting was such that he could also hit you at will!

PRAY WITH THE CHI
IN YOUR WILLPOWER

BEATRICE

Intellectual pygmies hated her logic.

Beatrice was a Karate student, as well as the most famous peoples' lib proponent in the old-time Greenwich Village days of my early Karate propagation history in New York City.

She had an incredible mind with no fear of anything. She was feared and respected by hostile schizophrenics. Intellectual pygmies hated her logic. Everyone else simply adored her. Over one hundred marriage proposals were made to her in her days. "Wow, what a girl."

These two people were teachers to me. I still feel small in front of them to this day. Arnold taught me what to do in life to succeed. Bernice taught me how to do it. That was the big difference between them.

Whereas, Arnold taught me how to fight real good, Beatrice taught me how to teach myself anything I wanted to learn real good. Arnold taught me how to hate people. Beatrice taught me how to understand others. Arnold taught me how to use people. Beatrice showed me how to utilize and improve myself. I am now convinced that people are the very best teachers for other people.

CARLTON

His lifestyle was his self-defense mechanism.

Coffin practice is totally unnecessary work....................

Carlton suffered from disorientation spells due to his fear of the outside world. "Agoraphobia (fear of the outside world), ruled supreme in his personal religion. It took me five years to teach him that the definition of the "outside world" is anywhere on the planet where a person is not alone. He had previously spent twenty-six years as a recluse living in a one-square block range of motion. It was necessary to cajole him sometimes to get out.

It was the fear of getting into a real fight alone that limited him to the distance he was not afraid to walk in during the daytime. His lifestyle was his self-defense mechanism. Agoraphobia is a very serious neurosis. Making him get out and train in my dojo was the therapy that cured him. I got him to view his twenty year term insurance policy as "death insurance." There really is no such thing in this world as life insurance. I consider one's fighting ability and one's weapons as one's life insurance We all need both. Carry your life insurance with you. Buy your death insurance from proper agents. He had health insurance, I told him that exercise and nutrition are the only health insurance, the Blue Cross and Blue Shield total medical coverage are for after the fact. That is to say sickness insurance. Going to the dojo every day made him happy.

Well, Carlton's lifestyle was definitely too high a price to pay for never having been taught how to fight real good in his childhood. He was a lightweight and a woman-hater. He wasn't homosexual, he was just beaten up by a girl. This happened in his youth, and he kept the "engram" (permanent burning memory) forever-after. I invented a legal personal weapon for him, because he couldn't relate to empty-hand fighting too good. I must say that he did have a lot of nerve, but not what you would call "real-guts" as a man. I respected him because he wasn't stingy and kept his word to me all the time. He did not shunt his debts in life.

I thank God in my middle-age now, that I had an uncle Jimmy who took me aside like a man when I was only seven years old. He took the trouble to teach me how to operate my hands as fists. He made me learn what to do, and how to feel in a fight. Uncle Jimmy's style as a man was that of a heavyweight boxer.

In essence, he taught me that "Hitting hard is the essence of fighting real good." Everyone should have an aunt or uncle who turns them on to something as useful as that. Well, that in effect is what I tried to do for Carlton. The only thing I wished for was that he could have started learning Karate as a very young child instead of a middle-aged man. His whole life would have been different and better. With adults and children, every Karate teacher must remember to never let training become a game. Too much sport attitude in the learning process of a serious subject like classical Karate training can make a youngster gravitate towards fantasy.

I taught Carlton that the inside world is wherever a person is "completely alone." Karate character is not best built in solitude. Words seemed to have quite an effect on Carlton. He was a very philosophical type of person anyway. He had an awful lot of girlfriends. His favorite line was, "I love you baby for what you are not." He also always gave them free pot. There is a lot to be said for bribery in that sense.

I rather think that he was loved more than he was respected. I convinced him that the "real world" by definition, is anywhere one is aware of not being in a box. The inside world equals "aloneness." The "outside world" is wherever you are not alone. "THE REAL WORLD IS WHEREVER YOU ARE!"

We are put in a box when we are born. It is usually called a crib or an incubator. Air gets pumped into an incubator. We all end up in a box of one type or another. It is usually called a coffin or an urn. I convinced Carlton that coffin-practice is totally unnecessary work.

DENISE

She thought that I was "stone cold" crazy for only the first year.

Denise used religion and disguises as her main self-defense mechanism. She always carried a bible and wore a large cross around her neck. Waitressing was the way she made her living. The gay quarter of old Greenwich village was her home ground. She had seventeen cats in a large loft. She was alcoholic as can be, and was deathly afraid of black women. She began taking Karate lessons upon the recommendation of her psychiatrist.

It took me three years of patient hard work to teach her how to fight, and particularly how to fight back. "Wow," what a difference three years of therapy made. I hypnotized her with words and encouragement, to the point that she just completely got bored her alcohol and cats compulsion. I convinced her that alcoholism was not a disease. I told her that she was lying to herself to give her an out. I called it being handicapped on purpose to avoid plain ol' work.

I told her that people fall in love with alcohol, because it is their best self-defense against a multitude of feelings. This is in-lieu of a physical self-defense against accepting the accurate world as the real one. She thought that I was "stone-cold crazy" for only the first year. I made her fight competitively in the women's' division of the America Cup Karate Championships. She did. She also won the first place as the winner for green belts and beat out a two-time winner, who happened to also be a black girl. Well, you can certainly see how that experience could help her.

Denise subsequently got herself a better job as a poetry-editor in Manhattan. She gave her cats, en-masse, to the high-executioner of the ASPCA; along with a donation of three hundred and eighteen dollars. She took a common-law husband and adopted two children. Her greatest moment in New York came when she finally got her own book of poetry published. Her two sons and one daughter are both already in a martial arts school. Denise wants them to be taught "how to fight real good" as children, so that hey will be ready to cope with high school in their precious teenage years. Kids, who do not learn how to fight, stay kids.

Remember: All begin at the bottom because the top becomes the bottom any other way.

ETHAN

I told Ethan that he and his wife were crazy.

Ethan's job was that of a taxi-driver. He always had horrible paranoia feelings along with his wife. I convinced him in only two years of Karate training that he was not afraid of people. He was afraid of the law. It seems that he and his wife were going along in life since they were eighteen without even filing an income tax. I brought out to them that this was the underlying cause of all their guilt. Such paranoia feelings would be with them no matter what they did.

No one can have the "clear-head" until they do things properly. Doing so would eliminate their nagging nauseating fear-feelings. You would be surprised at the number of poor young couples suffering from this mental handicap. Fear and guilt show themselves in every area of life for the same reason that confidence does. Confidence comes from what you do or are capable of doing. Fear comes mostly from what we don't or didn't do. Fear is easier than confidence, because it takes a lot less work-feelings.

I pointed out to Ethan that his job was particularly prone to putting a drive into a lot of paranoia feelings. It's an occupational hazard. Cashiers and liquor store clerks feel the same way about going to work every day too; for the same reasons.

Ethan mentioned that taxi drivers like to be called driver. They hate the word cabbies. They hate to be called "hey you."
Some women drivers won't even work the Bronx at night, according to many dispatchers. I told Ethan that he and his wife were crazy. No one in their right mind wants to work any night shift in the south Bronx; not even the police and the firemen. Ethan agreed that it would definitely help his wife's paranoia condition if he didn't insist anymore that she had to drive the cab on the night shift. "Wow, imagine having a spouse like him!"

Taxi drivers are famous for using everything from pistols, German-shepherd dogs, weapons in the visor, religious shrines, to locked-doors, as their main self-defense mechanism while they're driving. Some of them feign foreign accents and deliberately act stupid as well. Pulling one's ol' stupid act, or one's ol' crazy act, is not uncommon as a defensive maneuver by laboring people throughout the world.

Detroit city once had a cab driver who committed armed robbery on his passengers. He did it five times successfully in four weeks. He was then beaten to death by an irate ex-marine. It seems that the cabbies' hand-gun went click instead of blam. That's all the mariner's combat-experienced ears had to hear. He was taught how to fight real-good and he did.

FRANK

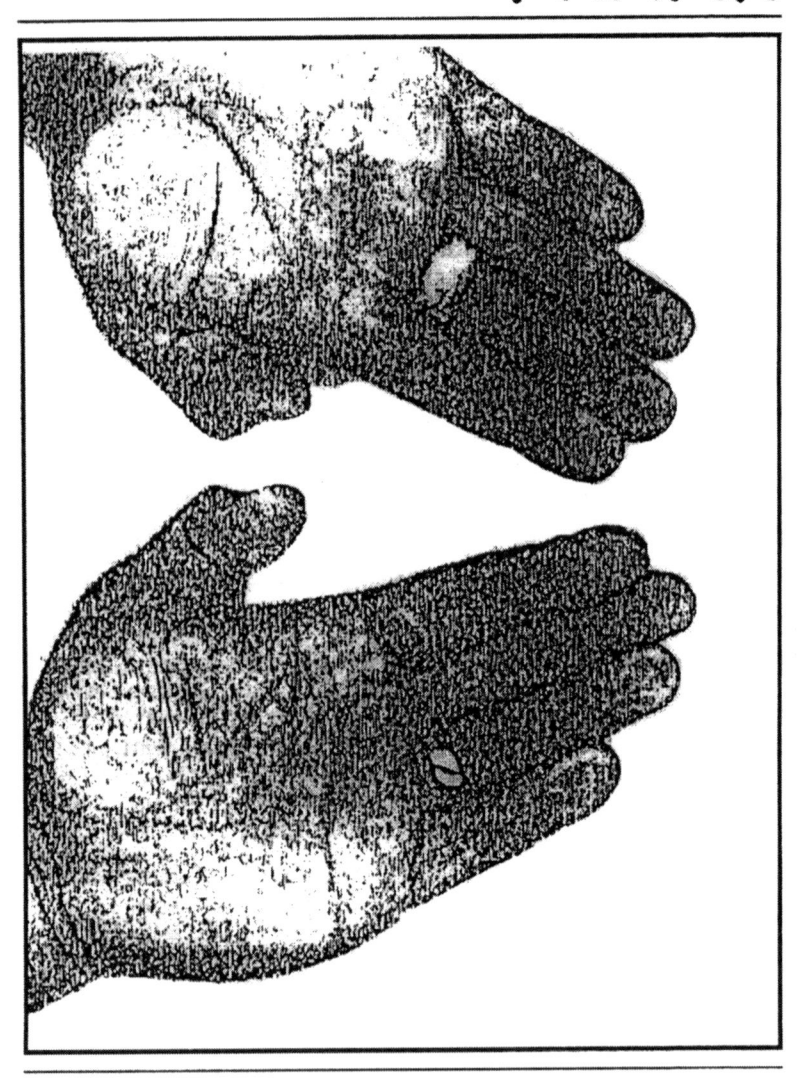

When I told Frank's father that it was illegal to carry an ice pick, he replied that it was illegal to mug a senior citizen.....

Frank's primary self-defense mechanism consisted mainly in hiding his face with glasses he didn't need. The kind that only looked good in the outdoors on a blazing-hot day or at the beach. His job was that of a post office supervisor. In three years of Karate schooling, I taught him how to fight real good. I hoped to cure him of barking at people, especially at work. His orders sounded like threats. This is the very best way to grow new enemies. Always acting like a tough-guy is a very inferior self-defense mechanism for a young man to pick for himself. TV role models are usually responsible. He agreed, and we went on to another matter.

I began to notice that the more his fighting ability grew in Karate school, the less and less the tough-guy mannerisms, with the voice to match, reflected themselves in the outside real-world of every day work. Frankie seemed surprised to learn that even the way we choose to act in every day life is related and integrated in our self-defense mechanisms. Again, I found "word-therapy" to be the strongest tool I had to work with in my teachings to my students. It is necessary to reach the mind before one can affect the body totally.

Frank's father was a night watchman, who had to

hand-check the doors of stores every night, through the streets of Little Italy and Soho in New York City. The old man had his working clothes such that he was never dressed twice the same way throughout the entire year. This was done as part of his disguises to keep from being mugged in his rounds. He also carried an icepick. It was holstered in his left inner-forearm. It was perfectly customized for his right handed underhand-draw. He worked a very dangerous job for a sixty-eight year old man. No young man in his right mind would go near that job.

When I told him that it was illegal to carry an icepick, he replied that it was illegal to mug a senior citizen. He had also studied fencing with the great Maestro Santulli. "Wow, what a self-defense mechanism." No wonder he had so much confidence for an old man in some of the most dangerous streets in the world.

Remember: The word of the Sensei is law by consent of the governed, because people rule themselves that way anyway.

GLORIA

She was a good bad girl and not a "bad good girl."

Gloria was a "good bad-girl," and not a "bad good-girl." That is her profile, and therein functioned her self-defense mechanism. I called it "Goodie tow-shoes-ism." Underneath her exterior of pure CW "femi-poo-isms" beat the heart of a cold-calculating sniper. She had two university degrees and three Karate black belt degrees all before she was thirty years of age. That was quite enough accomplishment it would seem to satisfy anyone's total self-defense mechanism. In Gloria's case it wasn't.

She was a chronic nail-biter from childhood. Parents, teachers and expensive analysts couldn't do a thing to cure her of this useless neurosis. It cost her one husband and one child, as well as five different teaching positions in a University. The years are not kind to those of us who may labor under the handicaps of costly neurosis milestone.

One day, I told her that one does not have to give in to all of one's feelings all the time. That one sentence caused her to stop nailbiting, drinking too much, and taking barbiturates, as well as amphetamine; as well as being a hard-core bi-sexual nymphomaniac. "Wow," what a mess that was.

I often plant idea seeds in my students' heads by

means of beautiful words. I call such words my psychological RX's. The subconscious minds of students always retain words that have the ring of accuracy for them. They ring the bell in the real world of the here and now like no other words ever could. The secret is to know the right words at the right time. That is not easy. In teaching, the discovery system is always the best. A good teacher always makes the student feel that every good idea for themselves was their's anyway.

Many years of birth-control pills finally brought on a clotting condition in the veins of her legs. It turned out to be quite serious. She was terrified of getting pregnant again. She saw her pills as self-defense mechanisms. They kept her from getting pregnant. She was paranoid without them. This made her become a celibate, as well as a recluse.

I pointed out to her that stupid fear feelings make people construct stupid defenses. She stayed in Karate until she was thirty-five years of age, and subsequently married another school teacher and lived happily ever after.

HARVEY

"Nowhereness............
Internal normlessness
"Anomie"

Harvey believed in magic. His self-defense mechanism consisted of living in "nowhereness." Wearing attention getting clothes and acting weird as a fruitcake all the time, was his "thing." I taught him that he was not an Oriental-holy man, and that, "That which is offered without proof, may be disputed without proof." That classical tid-bit was the psychological RX. I also let one of my sadistic brown belters beat the hell out him in the dojo's boxing-ring one summer night. Well, I thought for sure that he would quit training, but he stayed and studied for three years.

He started dressing like "normal-man" and got a civil-service job, only after I had him achieve confidence in his personal fighting ability. I taught Harvey that a wise man keeps his superiority to himself. He feigns stupidity and buries his goods deeply. It was necessary to use a lot of humor in that therapy, because he took himself to be endowed with super human abilities. He was an occult-nut.

I oftentimes run into a lot of females with that sickness. I call it "the ol' witch complex." The ol' sleeping beauty self image is the only thing I consider worse than that. Nothing beats having an accurate self image. The more accurate our self images are, the bigger and better they will be in the outside world.

I had to get Harvey to smile more often. I would say things like: "I taught you everything you know and you still don't know anything." He never totally gave up his basic belief in magic, but I did manage to convince him that one's ego must not be dependent upon what one does for a living. This is especially true if one sees oneself as a magician.

Harry Houdini had some trouble that way towards the end of his life. All good things come to an end, only when something better comes along. It always does. In other words, "The next one is always better." This means whether it is the next life, or the next job in life.

Harvey could scare people real good. I made him stop wearing his long cape. This happened when I said that he looked like an adjudicated lunatic. He didn't like being self adjudicated. He finally believed me when I told him that people do believe what they see most of the time.

IRENE

She was a looney girl in an all schizophrenic neighborhood in Brooklyn.

Irene used her fatness, deliberate ugliness, filthy language, pretended wealth, masculine mannerisms, and CW-unlimited: along with drugs to defend herself with. All of this in-lieu of a physical knowledge of how to fight real good with one's hands and feet. Needless to say, Irene was raised in a predominately "all macho" environment. She was a lonely girl in an all-schizophrenic neighborhood in Brooklyn.

It only took one year of Karate lessons to teach her how to fight well. The "shock-shove" technique of my Goju Karate is the most marvellous of all my therapeutic techniques. It particularly gives women super-normal hit-power in as short a time as possible; using instinctive and natural abilities. My lightweight-men and women adore that technique as having the most efficacy.

I noticed a direct correlation between the progress Irene made with a self-image change and her dropping all the ugliness in her life. She started to wear dresses for the very first time in her life. This was at the age of twenty-two. That's pretty late. She learned how to take care of her hair and use beautifully kept fingernails as a CW mechanism. She stopped dramatizing her tightness in dirty sawed-off short-shorts.

Irene lost her penis-envy syndrome when she learned through her Karate training that women who can fight better than men who can beat-up other men are taken seriously. Their words are listened to. She attracted a lot of lesbian social climbers in her circles. She accepted modern birth control methods as part of her self-defense mechanism, and not as an evil thing frowned upon by God. She stayed addicted to automobiles, cigarettes and pot, but totally forgot about alcohol and pills. I consider this an excellent success for just a year's Karate therapy investment in herself.

JEROME

He had the most severe case of the ol' bubonic laziness that I had ever seen in my life.

Jerome was a Karate student. He used poor health, asthma and perpetual poverty war stories as his main self-defense mechanism. He did this even in Karate school. I told him that his self-defense mechanism, as well as his self-image was quite stupid. It took me seven years of very hard Karate teaching to get him to a brown belt fighting level. Jerome was quite a slow learner. He didn't keep his body and clothing clean and neat. I made him finish high school by simply telling him that I would never consider him a brown or promote him to such until he had a real high school diploma first!

I convinced him that Shakespeare knew only one thing, and that was just twenty six letter of the English alphabet. The rest was up to Shakespeare himself. Jerome suffered from the most acute case of the bubonic-laziness that I had ever seen in my life. Parents, doctors and the United States marine-corps, as well as the ol' college dropout with even the dojo experience, failed to make a dent in his basic self-defense mechanism. The bubonic laziness itself, was his defense against everything. Some fancy doctors, costing the government and his parents a fortune, called it a psychologically induced asthmatic reaction syndrome due to the stress of not being able to cope.

WOW! Karate was his salvation. Without it, he would never have lived through the teens.

I found him to have no religion at all. My Karate was the closest thing in his framework of useful values. I taught him that worship, sacrifices, ceremonies, and praise are a self-defense mechanism in the universal sub-conscious of humans. It is used to defend against the fear of the wrath of God. I made him get rid of his "will to fail" to avoid work. I made him accept work itself, as the name of his personal religion. He had a bad habit of changing his name and phone number every two years, and losing his job every two weeks.

Every therapist of every discipline will have failures. Jerome is in his thirties now and is still a virgin boy. He's going around in circles, spending his whole life desperately trying to defend himself against the inevitability of being made to work by the "wrath of reality.

I taught him to consider God's name to be reality and he could not go wrong. Hallmark symptoms of the "bubonic-laziness" are revulsions to ablution therapy, unkempt-disheveled hair, sloppy clothes, always broke, never smiles and above all, never finishes anything. Sufferers of this disease have no war stories to be told about, as well as no future to be written about.

Ms. Kathleen

Her dealings with the outside world included for common law degree in advanced "vaginal politics."

Ms. Kathleen was the kind of beauty who stopped traffic. This was whether she was crossing the street, or walking into church. She was intelligent enough to realize that she used CW as her primary self-defense mechanism. CW is often called "circus-world" in some southern states in America. Her dealings with the outside world included for "advanced vaginal politics." She used its tactics, even though it wasn't really her game. I convinced her to learn how to fight real good. This was to get her the confidence necessary for her to put herself through college and have the strength necessary to live alone.

Her paycheck came from her secretary job. The Karate training kept bosses and supervisors from using her as just another receptacle for seminal fluid. That's a fact girls. Men are afraid of women who can fight real good. My catchy phrase was the key psychological R. It worked well on her mentality. She didn't actually hate men, but she didn't respect them either. She loved to call males pigs. She didn't even put the chauvinistic part in front of the key word.

I taught her to always wear a wedding ring on her left ring finger. This was even though she was legally single. Pretty girls get uptight feelings when waiting at bus stops, elevators, or out shopping. It comes from the vibes men and women project to all lovely objects of desirability. Men it seems, don't even go into "coming on strong gear" when that ol' reliable wedding ring is evident. Women do the same thing. Even diamond engagement rights don't carry the weight-mystique of "red lights" all the way, that the simple common gold wedding band does. Just ask yourself if you really know the meaning of the word shunting or not. Then come to your own conclusions. Karate psychology encourages speaking softly, carrying big sticks, and wearing your wedding right if you are married. Try it.

Wedding rings and tattoos are symbols of dedication. They are always flashing an aura of protection in an unspoken language. Kathleen's whole life changed when she started wearing a wedding ring as part of her self-defense mechanism. She actually saw it that way. Her obvious beauty was easier to defend. More large busted girls have to deal with the problem of largeness forever. They mostly become "mammary politicians."

Married men and women who do not wear their gold wedding ring, usually tell lies of how it interferes with their fingers someway, or keeps them from doing their job properly. People who do not want to feel married don't want to label themselves. They do not want to be known as not being on the market of liberty anymore.

Wedding rings inspire fear in predators. Rings are an excellent self-defense mechanism against telling lies. There are a lot of guys and dolls prone to getting themselves into unnecessary trouble in this world by fooling around with other people's property. This applies to all ages; especially to the geriatrics-set. People will wear phony glasses as masks. They will not wear the gold band of reality, however. Wedding ring wearers do have more fun in the real world. There is no shunting then.

LAURENCE

His total self-defense mechanism was money.

Laurence was a millionaire. His total self-defense mechanism was money. He used to hang out with the chess players and intellectuals of old Greenwich Village. The drug cult and the gay groups never took him seriously or knew he as not a poverty case. He acted too square. His mannerisms were that of a lonely workaholic family man. Laurence got turned on to physical health and self-defense at the age of forty. Since it is quite impossible to buy the confidence or robust health and individual fighting confidence, he began getting more and more into severe athletic fighting confidence. He loved handball bouts and Karate lessons at the YMCA. None of the local martial-artists could understand why a man with six million dollars would not be satisfied with himself just the way he was.

Well, he was struck down by a heart seizure in the hot summer while playing against men half his age. We read in the papers only six months after the funeral, that his beautiful wife had remarried his best friend. She had six million dollars to be happy with. Somehow it seems that we all learned a lesson from having known Laurence. We educated that vigorous handball competition was not a good therapy for loneliness or millionaires.

Ol' Laurence neither smoked or drank. His green Volkswagen sports car was as unobtrusive as his simple, casual, dressing habits. I was impressed by his black belt. It was really an ordinary looking leather trouser-type with no zipper compartments. A money belt is a beautiful self-defense mechanism. He played quite excellent chess. His favorite saying was, "Lord Chesterfield was an absentee daddy too." I knew what he meant by that, but I don't think any of the other guys at Sandolino's did. We all missed Laurence.

MONICA

She would have executed them both however, if she would have had my weapon and training then.

Monica valued her keyring weapon more than any material possession in the world. She took over ten years of serious Karate study. The weapon was a masterpiece of prosthetic perfection. I designed it to be invisible, silent, legal and to usefully serve a purpose, even when not in a self-defense use. I wanted to come up with something just as good for women. I like the idea of "soft-paw and hard-claw." It is my opinion that pound for pound, cats are the very best fighters in the world.

Monica, as well as sixteen other people to whom I gave this weapon, would not take any amount of money in the world for it. I mean this literally. I call it the Urban keychain parachute-ring. I have invested dozens of what I thought were infinitely superior self-defense mechanism tools, but little did I know the extent to which my students would value them. I have subsequently learned that most people value legal weapons more than legal money. Whenever I give people I like gifts, I always give them a labor-saving device or a self-defense mechanism. They love it.

Monica was a blind girl. She wanted to learn how to fight real-good, I found it interesting to note that she was raped by a blind man and woman couple. This happened when she was in her teens. Monica never became pregnant; she also never pressed charges. I really told her how stupid of her it was not to, but she was not quite psychologically ready to pull her own strings at that time in her life. There are millions of girls just like her all over the world. Another reason was that she was too afraid of retaliation. She would have executed them both, however, if she would have and my weapon and training then. I build and customize the weapon for each of my special students. Every project is a unique work of balanced perfection. I have never made an error in that area and never intend to.

The physical prowess confidence of Monica is such that she now feels that she can hit anything instantly. She is better than Zatoichi or Zoro within a three foot radius of her center. She can deliver enough foot pounds of force per square inch (hit power), to kill anything instantly at any time of the day of night. She loves her prowess more than food.

Needless to say, she also suffered from desire function. Nowadays we call that a-sexuality. I mentioned that a-sexuality is a self-defense mechanism against "letting-down the ol' guard." She believed that I was quite probably right about that. It seems everyone experiments with a-sexuality eventually. This is either out of necessity or to see where it goes.

Monica was a philosophical-type person. She believed that an advertised superiority is a weakness in any self-defense mechanism. That is why I call that statement Monica's law. I learned from her that unsighted people are more paranoid than sighted people are about the unknown. I used to tell her that fear vibes are just as detectable as smell.

Don't forget: Fainting at the sight of blood or at an autopsy as well as "swooning" passing out and getting suddenly ill, are all forms of shunting. Suicide is the grand ultimate shunting behavior exhibited by us humans. Animals and people can be suddenly frightened to death. This is a non-voluntary shunt. Certain sounds (Karate kiai) can frighten certain people and animals to death.

NICHOLAS

I taught him that people, as well animals and armies, react first to size and then to vibes.

Nicholas used his size all his life as his basic self-defense mechanism. I taught him that people, as well as animals and armies, react first to size, and then to vibes. This always happens whenever paths are crossed. Lightweights, who can beat up heavyweights, project vibes accordingly. Ol' Nick was a heavyweight. He was afraid of dominant lightweights. Size appreciation depreciates proportionately according to the lessening of the extent of the projected fear vibes. I call this Urban's third law of reality. It took me only one year to teach that to Nicholas. I turned him from a public punching bag on his garage job, to a respected, as well as feared two-hundred and forty pound class-A fighter of quality.

He learned about "gaze-control." I opened his eyes to the ol' arm around the shoulder buffaloing-tactics, and other con-mechanisms used by homosexual-type personalities. I taught Nicholas to translate the word personality to mean the person's style. The style of fighting always matches the personality of the person. I made him memorize everything through and including all the schools of thought on mind control I knew of. He excelled in that aspect of self-defense mechanism quite splendidly.

I found him to be an uneducated mechanical genius.

I got him to eagerly accept his real personality. This happened once he learned to fight real-good. I did find in my case histories that this sort of thing is far easier to do with men than with women and girls.

The elderly are the easiest students in the world to teach what to do. Getting them to actually exercise quite a bit impossible, outside of a large captive-group. Tai Chi Chuan activities are the best for that. The Chinese are the only culture in all history to have succeeded in getting it down pat. They compel group outdoor exercises in many old time communes. Much Chinese medicine does work successfully for tightly regimented and constricted societies.

I taught him to see that no one can ever be anything that they don't see and feel themselves to be in the first place anyway. A truthful self-image is the best self-defense mechanism. Big men look small to small men who can beat them up. Women react to the size of other women's breasts the way men react to the size of a other men's biceps. Large hands are always feared more than small hands. So too, is the case with Karate knuckles. All Karateists, particularly the very young ones, know that the large calloused punching knuckles are "some CW self-defense mechanisms" to have on themselves.

Such knuckles literally scare the hell out of everyone. Body builders' bodies do the same thing.

Longshoremen know how their hook, worn on the left shoulder of their leather jacket; quite legally of course, keeps even other longshoremen from "messing" with them. No one fools with the butcher in his shop. The closeness of all those beautiful killing, carving, slicing, stabbing, chopping, grinding, smashing, ripping and tearing tools, do in fact change the charisma of the atmosphere in the presence of such a person.

Claustrophobia is a form of useless paranoia to those who were never trapped. Nicholas was caught in an elevator during the second great New York blackout. Paranoia is a form of useless worry. It is best relieved with insurance policies. Paranoia is a form of negative feedback that should guide us and not control us. In order to know defense, it is necessary to first know what being attacked feels like.

"Have you ever been afraid?" That question is not nearly as interesting to ask a fighter as, "Have you every not been afraid?" Men who have not had the military experience host inferiority feelings when in the company of vets swapping war stories. All people who have not gone to college, feel inferior to diploma-holders. This is for the same reasons that common law wives feel inferior to properly certified marriage certificates holders. The same goes for common law divorces. There are advantages and disadvantages on both sides. So are common law educations.

Guys and gals on television interviews, or in run of the mill every day conversations in groupings, are never takes seriously anymore if they volunteer information to the effect that they have such and such a college degree, or black belt of one kind or another. Officer veterans still maintain a form of mind control superiority over enlisted veterans anywhere you may travel in this world. Karate therapy did not keep Nicholas from using his size mystique power in the total construction of his self-defense mechanism. It did, however, stop him from relying on it in the way that a neurotic person would. I taught him that large people who can not fight real good, do not feel large. Small people who can fight real good feel ten feet tall.

Remember: Everyone works because work means lives. They who have eternal work have eternal life. Our concept of death is "no more work." That is wrong! Paradise could not exist without work! Death is really one sophisticated way of changing jobs.

OPHELIA

Her favorite saying was "forgive and forget, but first get even."

Ophelia had no self-defense mechanism in life at all. She was first married at the age of fifteen to an alcoholic Yugoslavian fisherman. He often sodomized her, as well as battered her. Ophelia had one child and had to work as a laborer. An outdoor carwash in New Jersey worked her like a male horse. She started Karate school at the age of twenty; the baby was only five and had to be taken with her to the dojo and work. Ophelia proved to be what I call a unit-type "uneducated genius in survival."

She accomplished all the credits necessary for a brown belt degree in only one year of hard study and practice. Karate teachings opened her eyes and mind to the extent that she also got a new job and a new husband, in that order. She kept her son for herself.

I was most impressed by the way in which she got her divorce. She used implicit action psychology by physically back-kicking her first spouse directly in the bellybutton. She also body-slammed him into and through a kitchen dish cabinet. The divorce was uncontested. The judge granted it to her immediately.

A Japanese Judo teacher fell in love with her. They

lived happily ever after in Melbourne, Australia. The son joined the United States Navy. The mother and father went into the restaurant business. Ophelia's first husband ended up on the bowery in New York City. He passed away from freezing to death in an abandoned slum.

Ophelia's favorite saying was "forgive and forget, but first get even." I always told her that the reason perfect pencils have perfect erasers is because there are no perfect people. She believed that patience was never being early. I found that to be memorably impressive to me.

Her incredible punctuality even exceeded my own military habits. Punctual people and neat people never take sloppy or always tardy persons seriously. Neats get along with other neats because they have everything in common. A common neurosis is better than nothing in common at all.

The sloppy, always late type of person, hates to live with another of their own ilk because no one ever does the work. No one keeps the house together and clean. Sloppy cooks, however, for some unknown reason; probably a lack of neurosis, make better tasting food than the super neat and clean type. The best self-defense mechanism against ever getting stuck in life with a sloppy, dirty, lazy roommate, is prejudice. All neat people hate to live with sloppy people.

Ophelia was neat as a pin. I attributed some of that to the Judo training of her day. The teachers of those days were Japanese influenced perfectionists. It showed in the personalities of the students and even affected their ways of doing things. They believed that "Perfectionism is the essence of beauty." That's a hard code to live by. It only works in the military.

PAUL

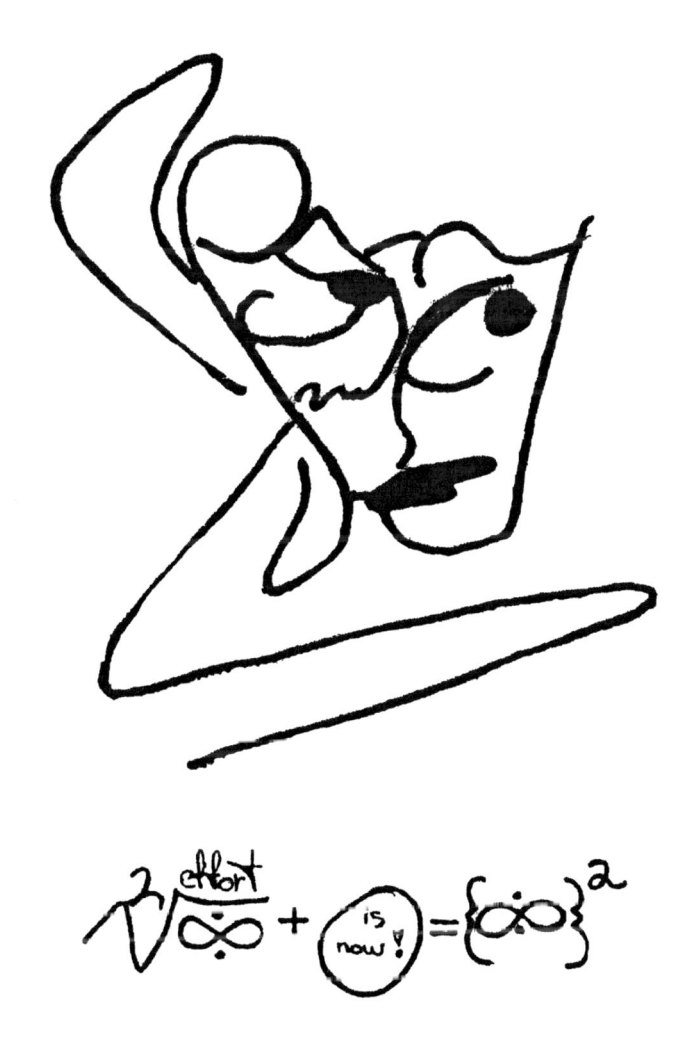

$$\sqrt[3]{\frac{effort}{\infty}} + \left(\overset{is}{\underset{now!}{}}\right) = \{\dot\infty\}^a$$

His favorite saying was, "The origins had no Universe."

Paul had the perfect self-defense mechanism. It was the total lack of the will to fail. I had never before in my life met with that type of person. He never took chances. He felt that safety was an engineered thing. He never missed one day of school - ever. This means from Kindergarten through the end of college. He also never missed even one day or one minute, or any hour of work in his whole life.

Paul believed in saving money from the age of nine. He married perfectly on the first time around. His children were perfect university material. He owns his own home and car. He commanded respect and not love or fear from everyone in his world. He finished two university degrees in night school before reaching thirty years of age. In short, he could outwork any five men, any time, or in any place. He fought the way he worked.

Paul was my concept of a perfect workaholic. He commanded one hundred and fifty employees. He got things done like a chief boatswain mate. He often told me that the hardest job in the world is the work of getting other people to work properly. All a coach, or a priest, or a teacher, really does, is get workers to keep doing their work.

His loved ones will never know what poverty is. He is legitimately happy and has been so since childhood. (A real "homo-normals.") Everyone was afraid of his will-power. Paul was stocky and defined "mind-control" as self-control. He learned all of the Karate technology I was capable of teaching him in only one and a half years. I have never seen anything like that before.

Paul can still fight better than all the middle-aged men I know. Every therapist will eventually run into a Paul type. It certainly is more than just refreshing when it happens. Paul earnestly believed that skills are transferable, and that anyone who reads too much can not write. "Wow," what a statement.

His favorite saying was "The origins and no universe." He also said, "Without en passant, chess would not be interesting." Anyone who plays chess, should play to win only, or the game lends itself to the cultivation of fantasy.

He was a relatively slow mover. His secret was mastery of pace. He didn't let his opponent/player lead or influence his own pace in the slightest. It something like one boxer trying to get or goad the other fighter into burning his own energy up too fast. "Rope-a-dope" is rather like that analogy.

He claimed that chess was essentially a sad-masochistic means of contact; not unsimilar to the feelings hosted by compulsive gamblers. Paul never gave anyone lessons, tips, or secrets. He considered his secrets in chess-play as his personal self-defense mechanism against losing.

QUANTA

She had the soul of a woman and the punch of a man.

Quanta was a Ju-Jitsu girl. She also studied Karate for two years. He whole life was spent in northern Italy. She had a scar-marked face with short butch hair, and was perfectly fluent in Italian, English and German. She did not like French or mathematics. She was not afraid of men because of having trained in a next door classical dojo since the age of five. All Italian parents believe in giving their kids martial-arts training.

Quanta was a chain smoker who did believe in God, but never made a spectacle of it. She used to work, once in a while, for very good money as a female body guard. She was such a good fighter that men would hire her to accompany them. It was not as a sex companion, but as a real live bodyguard. She did not carry a gun, but did know how to best use an ice-pick and a strangulation cord. She was very adept at the "silent-kill," and the use of the secret and elite bolo cord neck weapon. I definitely thought she was weird, but not at all schizophrenic in behavior.

I knew her for a long time while I was teaching and propagating Goju in Italia. That country is full of intriguing little things like that. Paranoia runs rampant in the everyday life of even just ordinary working people.

I was extremely interested to learn about the clandestine knife fighting schools in southern Italy. There was also an amazing school where students went for six months (twenty four hours per day) of live-in training. They came from all over the world at the incredible cost of one hundred and eighteen thousand dollars a piece. They came from high echelon circles of foreign governments and big corporate businesses. Needless to say the teacher only took six students per year.

Quanta had the soul of a woman with the punch of a man. Her body-language mannerisms were that of a boy. She never smiled and had a Marlene Dietrich-sounding voice. I thought she was somewhat sexy, but to the Italians, she was frightfully too masculine. Macho-ism is a form of CW that men understand in the behavior and personalities of other men, but "femi-poo guys" alienate everyone. Quanta was a tough girl.

Body guarding is a highly paid prestige profession in Italy for Karate dans with university degrees, preferably in psychology and industrial engineering. Body guarding is really the world's oldest profession. It was the main way Samurais made their living in old Japan. Italian youth drop out of school only for poverty reasons, none of them ever gets the bubonic-laziness when it comes to knowing the value of education. They highly respect education and teachers and applaud teachers and professors.

Quanta's favorite saying was, "What the hell are you talking about?" She could not cook, but had developed a perfect middle-weight body. She became quite famous in the martial-arts world of Padova. I classified her as a feminine butch type. She would not let you down in a fight. Girls who can fight real-good make valuable friends.

Remember: Nothing is free because it costs time. There is nothing else!

ROGER

He did have the unique ability of being able to break people's spirits without having to break their backs in the process.

Roger believed that systematic-logic and creative imagination can originate any universe. He as a planner for a tremendous world wide corporation. His main self-defense mechanism was the intelligence that a superb education and an uncompromising loving father could induce in a man. Roger studied Karate for two years. His Ph.D. was in political-science. You could call him the kind of person that no one crosses or fools around with. It is interesting to note that, Humphrey Bogart, John Wayne, and Frank Sinatra were that way in real life. His personality reminded one of those types. He could also use a gun real good to defend himself with. He saw the world as a very tough place. Roger had no weakness with weaklings. His favorite word was, "No!"

He did not like to play chess. He could converse on a top level in Italian, English, Spanish, German, French and Greek. "Wow, what a self-defense mechanism." A person who can speak more than one language, can be more than one person. There is a lot to be said for the ability to function perfectly in more than one cultural milieu. Such people seem to derive energy and confidence from just themselves.

I refer to such personalities as "self-starter people." Your religion gives you that.

Roger also had the military experience in the Italian Air Force. He served as a captain. He considered civilian life in Italy to be more natural and challenging. Military careerists can live a full life; and learn to save money, to possibly become thousandaires. They could never become millionaires. Real gung-ho military type guys and gals see civilians as some sort of inferior species. That is inordinately interesting.

He did have the unique ability of being able to break people's spirits without having to break their backs in the process. He could have been a superb Sensei of Karate, but money came first in his life, always. He was a fabulous after dinner speech maker. He always opened with the beautiful words, "In this moment of seriousness." I never met anyone who would want him for an enemy. Class-A corporate executives like that believe implicit actionists make the best planners and inherit the earth.

His favorite saying was, "The purpose of work is to make money. Don't rationalize it don't intellectualize it, don't venerate it, just do it, more and more, everyday in every way, to make more and more money." He took pride in having studied in the same classroom as Gallileo.

He had a flat on the same block that Shakespeare once lived on. Great pride is taken in that sort of thing in Italy. Roger was a chain smoker. He believed in garlic therapy for a healthy constitution. His tobacco habit and his dandruff were the only things he didn't like about himself.

SUSAN

Her main self-defense mechanism was God.

Susan believed in Jesus. Her main self-defense mechanism was God. She believed in turning the other cheek and forgiving enemies. I taught her to respect her friends, love herself, and punish her enemies! I had to teach her to turn the other cheek, with a spinning Karate chop to her enemy's throat. She would not buy "that religion" of mine. I did like her favorite saying, which was "You've got to feel a thing before you can do it."

Her bad traits were that she wouldn't study how to fight real good with her hands and feet. She honestly counted completely on her religious belief that God alone would always keep her safe from physical harm. She was famous for the size of her large family. There was no other topic of conversation ever on anything in her house, other than Jesus.

She studied Karate with me for only four sessions. I broke out one day and told her point-blank, "You have to want to learn to fight real-good with your hands and feet doing the dirty work to survive in the outside world. God will not do the work for you that you are too lazy to do for yourself."

She kept trying to convert me. I saw it as her excuse to avoid seeing any other thought or feeling any other things that was not compatibly on-going with her continuing neurosis. My favorite saying for her therapy was, "People don't feel what you see! It's a big world out there." Susan shunted everything to keep her world safely small.

She did not like Karate or the women's lib movement. She ran a matriarchal home. She and her husband did have adjacent spontaneous remission experiences in regards to their concomitant quitting of chain smoking however. It was amazing. They never resumed the habit. The funny part that I remember so vividly is that they did not suffer any withdrawal syndrome at all.

I can not help but feel that there is a lot to be said for Susan's religious world. I told her that most people take their religion as a very private and personal thing. One should not make it the topic of everything all the time. It cheapens it when there is nothing else. My therapy didn't work on her. The superiority feelings she exuded when dealing with people in the outside world were such that no real communications of an interpersonal type could be established. I call this not having contact.

Love is a form of perfect contact. This is even if it is temporary. Talent is a form of natural perfect contact with a discipline. Religion is contact with one's beliefs. One does something with one's religion as if it were a tool or a weapon. One's religion or tool, or weapon, or education, does not do something with you. Remember that!

Susan's husband was a Pentecostal minister. He would not agree with any of my beliefs. Karate is motion plus emotion. The religious experience is an emotion. It goes very well with the motion of work. I tried to teach them that prayer alone was not as useful as prayer plus work. They thought I was sinful.

Remember: Hunger is a form of pain. Boredom is a form of pain. The essence of the depression feeling is nothing more or less than a total loss of a belief in a future potential.

SAVING MONEY IS PAINFUL.

TIMOTHY

He was killed in the streets three years later in a gang fight.

Timothy loved his guns most of all. I told him that, "They who live by the gun, die by the law!" His self-defense mechanism was directly related to his drug addiction. Intense paranoia is the natural crash that hard-core addicts are used to paying for their unnatural high with. It's an awfully high price to pay for anything.

In the old days, before law and order were everywhere, those who lived by the sword died by the gun. Those who live by the needle die by their own hand. There was no Karate teacher in his right mind, who would accept Timothy into their dojo. The dojo for the Karate teacher is the psychological operating room. The self-defense mechanism is analyzed, reconstructed, improved upon and in some cases torn down there.

Timothy was sixteen years old when I first smacked him in the mouth. This was in front of his mother. I had to also take his pistol from him.

I got his family to get him enrolled in the methadone program. This is the only therapy I could think of at the time. I knew that he would never work or learn how to fight real good like a man should. He had no father image to grow up with. I'm surprised that his

poor mother didn't loose her mind trying to raise him. There was also a daughter headed in the same direction.
I gave Timothy a Doberman while he was an outpatient at St. Vincent's. This therapy did more good than physical beatings ever could. The dog gave him confidence, identity and responsibility. It lessened the fear his mother and sister had to live with in their poverty environment. Poverty and paranoia always go hand in hand. So do drug addiction and alcoholism. Alcoholism is drug addiction.

Timothy was a Chinese kid. He lived in an Italian neighborhood on Mott street. He was very lucky to be alive, because even the Chinese street gangs would have nothing to do with him. I saw Timmy five times in five years. Each time, I gave him an inspirational talking to. It did no good. He was killed in the streets three years later in a gang fight.

The one great advantage Karate Senseis have over conventional therapists is that the Karate or Kung-Fu teacher doesn't have to send the student to the hospital for shock-therapy. The student goes to the hospital after the therapy to get patched up. Timothy was a natural born actor. He was also a polished con-artist. I believe that such people can not be cured or controlled. They can be contained.

The therapy of mainland China for such cases is: "Get well or get killed." It is a very realistic approach to life.

URSLA

She was over thirty years of age and never had a sex experience.

Ursla was a ballet teacher. She was about the most normal student I ever had. She possessed absolutely no self-destructive habits. She got along in Karate very well with Paul. I still have a suspicion; after all these years, that they were secretly making it on the side. A lot of that sort of thing used to be the vogue in the old days. I refused to allow that in all my dojos through the years.

Ursla had an absolutely perfect body for ballet. That is what made her Karate katas so fluid. Her round-kick and cat-stance were absolutely perfect. She took two years of Karate lessons. She practiced her yoga exercises every morning. Honesty and simplicity were the main self-defense mechanisms in her character. Ursla was swift, lithe and strong. In middle-age, she could kick, and move better, and with more gracefulness than any of the young champions in America (circa 1965 N.Y.C.).

She came to Karate training because she wanted to learn "hit-feelings." Ursla wanted a discipline that taught one how to express anger feelings realistically. She was over thirty years of age and never had a sex-experience. "Wow, no wonder she felt that she was not expressing or experiencing her entire range of human emotion."

She became a skilled fighter quite soon. This demonstrated and proved to me that skills are entirely transferable. I suspected that Paul took care of the lack of her sex-experience needs. Anyway, I guess they were both mature enough to not need philosophical-psycho-analysis from me on that subject.

I got her to be able to express anger in less than half a year. This was done by making her compete in the fighting competitions. She was afraid of getting hurt. I taught her that the difference between the martial-arts and most other arts was that in the martial-arts, it was necessary to take the chance of getting hurt sometimes!

It is the only way to learn the motional and emotional skills and attitudes it takes to keep from being hurt in the real world of violence. She always wore dresses while living with her mother. They had three Great Dane dogs. I considered them to be a terrific self-defense mechanism. They lived alone in lower Manhattan. They never got robbed or raped. Large dogs and property owners go very well together.

Remember: The work of the Sensei is the word of the Sensei.

VICTOR

He used hate as his main self-defense mechanism.

Victor used hate as his main self-defense mechanism. He projected hostility vibes to the extent that most people were afraid of him. This included even his parents. He came to Karate school on the recommendation of his older brother who was a black belt in Judo. Victor had done a lot of "jail-time" in his youth. It definitely showed.

Victor soon learned that all his weird behavior, sullen face, abrasive personality and buffaloing techniques, simply did not work with even adolescents half his age. Victor was a born loser. He was punched right in the face on his first day in Karate school. One of my female black belts did it. She knocked him out cold because he deliberately tried to hurt her in basic practice. "Wow!" did he ever learn a lesson about what a truly practical self-defense mechanism was.

Bad vibes subsequently began to disappear from Victor's behavior patterns. He eventually became normal. I watched his progress very carefully to see if he would turn out to be a bully, once he got the ability to fight real good. He stuck the discipline of Karate out for two years. He learned that Karate people are specialists in violence. They have no need for phony attitudes.

Victor never became a great fighter. He did become a super normal person, however. He stopped bullying weaker people. Karate school makes super normal out of the normal, and normal out of the sub-standard. I have a feeling that the girl who punched him in the face that day did him a favor. Shock therapy was a gift in that case. It was the immediacy of her implicit action that did the most good in waking Victor up to reality.

He did have some good traits. They came out as his attitude towards others in the world normalized. His chess game was inordinately brilliant for his lousy personality. He played pool like a shark. This redeemed him a bit with my Karate group.

Victor could draw well and speak perfect German. He was a tall middleweight. He eventually passed the entrance exam to become a transit cop. Victor married a school teacher, whose life he saved while responding to a shooting incident in Astoria. His favorite saying was "Discipline is made of iron, self-discipiine is made of rubber." I had to agree.

Remember: Insane people do not know they are so when they are doing their insane act. Neurotics do not know they are neurotics. When people do their crazy act on purpose, it is not insanity, it is tactics and strategy of some kind, and part of their self-defense mechanism. The next time you see persons doing their crazy act, look at it that way and see what you see.

WANDA

Her main desire was to kill Adolph Hitler.

Wanda used African voodoo as her main self-defense mechanism. "Wow, I couldn't get over it." She was convinced that she was a witch. She wore a cape, long blond hair, and could scare the hell out of people with her voice and eye changes. I totally dislike scary mystique types of personalities. She could literally read minds. I mean for real! She interpreted body language and vibes language like a pro.

As a woman with a super large body, she had no qualms against punching people in the face. Wanda claimed that she was really a man trapped in a female body. I found that concept of herself to be rather cliche, but I took it as serious data anyway. Wanda sincerely believed that persons could live forever if they really wanted to. Her intentions of going on to 201 years of age before she would want to "change worlds" really dumbfounded me. I couldn't take her seriously anymore after that.

She made her living as a health food store owner. There were many times when I thought she was crazy as a looney tune. I wouldn't buy anything in that store once I started to chart all her idiosyncrasies. She studied Karate earnestly with me for two years. She took Tai-Chi-Chuan for five years. Women in general were always frightened by just the sight of her. As a little girl, she played alone in a cemetery located near the home in which she grew up. At the age of fifty she took her first Karate lesson. This quite impressed me.

Wanda's only regret in life was that she could not serve in World-War 2. Her main ambition was to kill Adolph Hitler. Most of her enemies were Hitler type amphetamine addicts. She, surprisingly enough to me, definitely was not a drug user of any type, other than food. That is what got me more interested in health food people. I figured there might be something of value to learn from them.

She was not in the least bit afraid of hostile schizophrenics. They were her speciality. People were afraid to cause problems in her store. I told her that they were reacting to her image and vibes and not to her. I do think that she was quite rude more times than the occasions demanded. I personally never condone rudeness with implicitness.

Although, she was born, raised, and educated in Italy, her aura was not of this planet. She would make a great friend for anybody and a terrible enemy for everybody. She had absolutely no racial prejudices. She liked to pick up black guys and sailors when she was a young college girl. She hated marriage and children. I always wondered why.

Wanda was absolutely against cigarette smoking. Her favorite saying was, "Smoking dehumanizes people and contributes more to forming a neurotic viewpoint than anything else in the world." "Wow, what a statement."

XANTOS

He was a physical fitness fanatic who became a loan shark in civilian life.

Xantos used money as his self-defense mechanism. Dollars were bullets to him. He was the kind of person who bought everything and paid for nothing. Each person in his world fell into his web of manipulation and counter manipulation. He made slaves out of people without them even knowing it. He knocked his first man out with a blackjack at the age of nine.

Xantos studied Karate in Okinawa for four years. He rose to the rank of major in the marine corps, as well as saved ten-thousand dollars by the time he was thirty years old. All people in his world feared his money and respected him.

He was a physical fitness fanatic who became a loan shark in civilian life. He married a girl from my Karate school. She could fight real good and did not come from a poverty situation. He was fifty years old at that time. She was a nineteen year old black belter.

I once told him that money wasn't everything. He told me that I was wrong. I then asked him whether or not he would ever trade his fighting ability for a million dollars. He said not. I asked why. He then replied, "It's not enough money."

His favorite saying was, "Life is a forced march." Xantos adopted the Greek orthodox religion, but did not believe in having children. He invested his money in real estate only. He kept more than one safe deposit box full of green money.

I found him to be quite interesting as a person. There was no excitement in his personality, however. He could play a wicked game of chess. Morphy was his hero. I definitely envied his self-defense mechanisms. I confided to him that I was going to write books to make money with for my old age. He replied, "There is nothing else." I subsequently made those words into my favorite saying for myself.

Remember:
A loss of faith in the here to come =
Depression.
A loss of faith is the here and now =
Fear.
A loss of faith in the there and then =
Enlightenment.

YOLANDA

She became a madam in her thirties.

Yolanda used CW as her chief self-defense mechanism. She definitely was psychologically in trouble as a person. I called her a stone cold charismatic schizophrenic, who if it wasn't for two years of Karate school therapy, would have gone mad or got herself killed. She had a crazy lifestyle as a professional prostitute.

She became a madame in her thirties. Even eighth avenue pimps were afraid to mess with her due to her Karate training. She had a statuesque body with a Eurasian personality. Her courage was that of a wolverine. I found her mind to be quite brilliant. She hated chess and rhetoric. Her singing voice was marvelously unique. She also mastered all of men's weaknesses. If it weren't for drugs, she could have been a superb school teacher in any solid small town, U.S.A.

Yolanda knew every feminine mystique technique in the book of secrets. He mind control was as strong as any man's. She loved poetry, dogs, cats, singing and cooking. Her sense of the dramatic impressed everyone, even in Karate school. A Cadillac and a mink coat were her favorite material possessions.

She was definitely not stingy, but always made more

money than she spent. I found her to be rather religious with many unfathomable superstitions. I made her aware of how her reliance on CW would not work in her world as the years went by. I made her take a course on thanatology (study of death and endings of life) and aging. That as her schizophrenic side.

Her philosophy was: "It is best to be feared in the arena of work, loved in the bedroom of romance, and respected in the world of reality." I found those to be very beautiful words. I kept them for my Karate teachings. I told her that her philosophy alone, was an excellent self-defense mechanism in itself; worthy of being a religion.

Her favorite saying was, "Something is better than nothing, only when it is not poison." I don't know where she got that one, but I nodded in agreement over it. She loved Tom Jones' music and Abraham Lincoln portraits. Black lovers and Greek food made her happy. She believed in spending heavy on good food. "Wow, what an unusual person!"

Remember: The very word "competition" scares young teenagers and other students. Survival is competition! Karate psychology teaches us that. Only death is a "no-more competition!"

ZIGGI

He could cloud people's minds.....

Ziggie's self-defense mechanism was abstract terminology. He could cloud people's minds with rhetoric to the extent that everyone felt inferior in his presence. He learned how to fight real good from Chinese Kung-Fu Sifus in Hawaii in the nineteen thirties. He was born of racially mixed parents with an Oriental philosophy and a Christian religion.

The mandarin mannerisms he evinced went very well with his degrees. He earned three doctorates and eight martial-arts levels. What a self-defense mechanism! Imagine, dear reader, all of that, and multilingual as well. He believed that Karate was the best universal language understood anywhere in the world.

He was fond of saying, "Everyone and anyone, understands all pain and violence." His concept of the classical man could not include for the lack of the ability to fight real good. He did not believe in magic, but could do magical things with people. He commanded the total respect of the very best Karate Senseis in the world.

Ziggie believed that fear came before the self-defense mechanism. Man's first important knowledge had to be "how to survive real good." He maintained that we had to defend against the temperature; against hunger and the furried, taloned and clawed beasts, to whom we were the favorite food. We, as people, have developed our best self-defense mechanisms to defend ourselves from our own kind. "The how to fight real good necessity," preceded all other knowledge it would seem. Our very existence is the proof of that. Farming, hunting, working, praying, are all results of the original need.

Starvation had to be defended against. Fighting and killing preceded mathematics, language, fire and the wheel. All of these things came later and only amplified man's ability to fight and kill in a super normal manner. His speeches and analogies always impressed everyone.

Karate Senseis take pride in realizing that the self-defense mechanism was the first knowledge. That is why we take that aspect of life so seriously. We tend to interpret life and living in terms of being a form of self-defense mechanism, in one way or another; for literally everything. Karate mentalities are not a bit romantic it seems.

It is good to remember: "A Karate person in training, is in Karate. Strength comes from health. Speed comes from effort. Technique comes from experience. Willpower comes from faith (in the self)." It is interesting to notice that serenity comes from old knowledge and fascinating to conclude that progress comes from new knowledge. Serenity is not the great thing some ancients used to think it was. That is the reason Arthur Fiedler worked himself to death. Eighty four is just another number to creative people. He died at that age. He loved his work best.

**PEOPLE WATCHING
IS BETTER THAN A LIBRARY.**

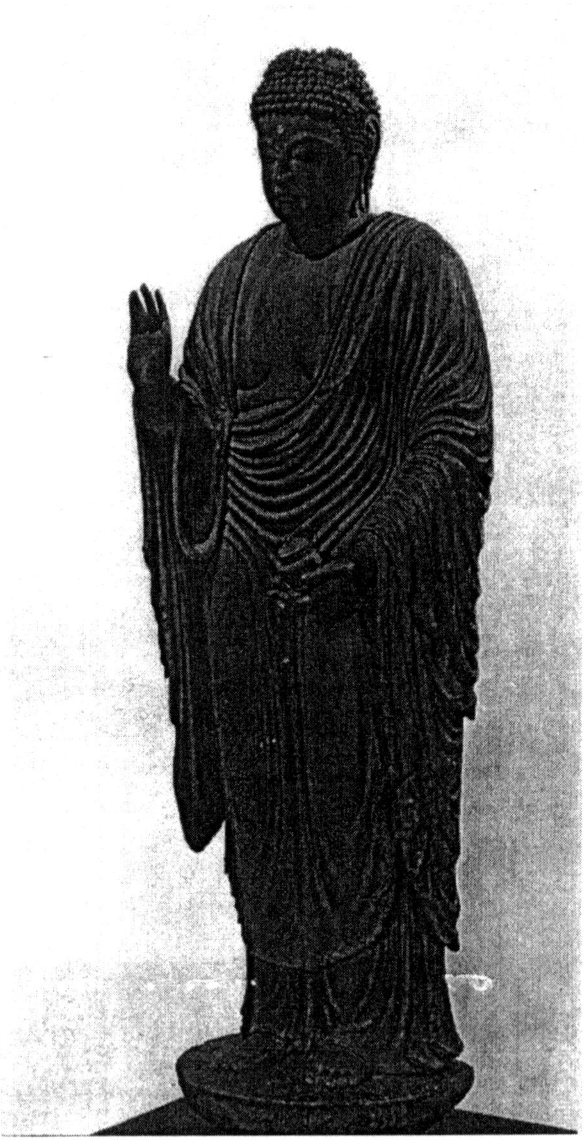

GUIDELINES FOR SELF-ANALYSIS

Individual Karate men are a composite picture of the below listed characteristics. It continually changes as the various breakthrough points in Karate development occur. The object of the true Karate man is to achieve as many class "A" characteristics as possible. This lifetime practice is the true meaning of Karate as a way of life.

A

Harmonizes hard and soft
Efficient
Tournament fighter
Quick to seize opportunity
Lives Karate daily
Looks, acts and feels sharp
Lives in reality
Knows nothing is free
Blocks soft, hits hard
Self controlled
Knows self
Works for a better life
Never breaks training
Learns from everything
Seeks happiness from inside

Relies on self
Gets better with age

B

Separates hard and soft
Compulsive
Won't get involved
Wastes time
Rationalizes
Part time person
Only when in the mood
Relies on others
Practices false economy
Overcompensates with feet
Loses control
Magnifies self
Lives for a better work
Has no future
Doesn't listen to others
Seeks happiness outwardly
His word means nothing
Gets weaker with age

C

Knows no soft
Restricted
Is afraid of competition
Has no patience
Doesn't know difference
Will drop Karate too

Has no feelings
Is disoriented
Loves poverty
Can't experience anger
Will fold in Jiu-Kumite
Underestimates others
Is afraid of work
Has no faith
Will not read
Waits for happiness
Has no friends
Gets smaller with age

Class "A" Lightweights

Speed and endurance
Big threat at close quarters with elbows and knees
Likes to hit and run
Utilizes circular motion
Develops many combinations
Attacks in bursts
Perfects jumping backhand
Will wear opponent down
Operates well in cat stance
Never skips makiwara
Fights viciously
Most spectacular style
Builds, defines muscles,
powerful calves and forearms
Never skips meals
Never dissipates

Class "A" Middleweights

Versatility and long range
Attacks face with jump kicks and round kicks
Likes to dance and sharpshoot
Will harass, sweep and trip
Perfects back kick
Dances and feints
Perfects lunge punch
Will suddenly change pace
Operates well in horse stance
Never skips kata

Fights relentlessly
Most interesting style
Builds elongated muscles, broad shoulders, flat gut
Keeps balanced diet
Always exercises

Class "A" Heavyweights

One punch knockout power
Always ends fight at close quarters
Likes to grab and hit
Will slug it out
Develops big Kiai power
Stalks
Perfects blocking systems
Will study opponent first
Operates well in sanchin
Never skips jogging
Fights ruthlessly
Most popular style
Builds massive chest, big fists and strong feet
Aware of rest and nutrition
Puts health first

TODAY IS NOW!

CONCLUSIONS OF A TENTH DAN

A super normal individual will have a full range of motion and emotion choices available to him or her. Such a person is consistent, but not inflexible. The sub-standard individual does not have a full range of motion and emotion choices available to him or her by personal choice. There are no patron saints for them.

It is my opinion that super-normal is better than normal. I believe that normal is better than sub-standard. It is usually ignorance of one kind or another that defines limited choices.

Each individual has his or her own particular style of behavior. It is different from others and not interchangeable. I call these things "quirks."

An adherence to only one's own view is neurotic when it does not work successfully all the time. The super-normal person does not have such limitations imbedded in his or her personality. The neurotic individual labors under handicaps of viewing imaginary restrictions as real.

Differences in behavior are possible because the

outside world does not always see what the inside world feels and conversely the inside world does not always feel what the outside world sees.

I am convinced that the real world is reality and as such, is an outside thing not subject to interpretation. I am fond of calling that the sublime undifferentiated absolute. I view the laws of gravity that way.

The process of human behavior could theoretically be programmed, but not accurately predicted. To be able to predict all human behavior accurately, would constitute an inordinately powerful weapon. It would allow the professor of such a power to control other people on a scale larger than that which could be accomplished by conventional modern weaponry. Some say the television sets in our lives are that already. Television can induce behavior which can statistically measure afterwards, but not accurately predicted. Out elections show that. Mathematics is the only accurate thing in the universe we have to work with. It was discovered and not invented. The mathematician reports on accuracy in the real world. The writer reports on everything.

It is good that the quality of human behavior can be manipulated. I like living in a world where every person, place or thing is equally real. This also applies to mental processes and emotions. It is good that non-neurotic persons to be accurately labeled as such. This applies even if it is not at the same time, to be acceptable as a judgmental opinion from other non-neurotic persons.

I have concluded long ago that a good self-defense mechanism makes greater freedom for one. Humans have greater choice ranges than all other species of life on this planet, ergo are capable of vastly more viciousness and sadism to their personal purposes in reality.

Vulnerability and cowardice are not necessarily characteristics of humans, but become so in the neurotic example. I took great delight in bringing this out in prose form with my twenty-six letters of the English alphabet case histories of this report to you. I depicted them in incrypted form. Some of the shoes from some of the cases can probably fit most of us sometimes. Everything really happened the way I wrote about it, I simply scrambled the chronology, names and other things that could possibly pinpoint accurate identity ever. I got the idea from the middle ages writer social protesters. They would use things like "Hickory Dickory Dock" rhymes to say almost anything. It works universally. We use songs today.

I have found, so far, that plant life can not make choices. I like discovering that thorns, needles and other things are used by them as a self-defense mechanism for the individual species. The spider's web, killing abilities, wrapping, tying and storing other insects for food, really impressed me. I have met people who behave the same way. I have met people who feel the same way about plants. They believe that plants do emit measurable vibrations. This also excites my curiosity to further pursue my studies of self-defense mechanisms.

I was fascinated to conclude that sadism is solely human, and is accompanied by an internal restriction, such as to cause depersonalization or schizophrenic distortion. This handicaps us as people more rapidly than all our other international neurotic processes. I feel that my conclusions on self-defense mechanisms are quite accurate to me. I only hope that more than half of my readers concur. Time will tell.

There is no question, but that internal, or personal expansion is more rapid in those of us with occasional environmental change for the good, than it does with reclusive neurotics, shut-ins, and the handicapped elderly, who stay home all the time. They can get institutionalized quite easily. Fearfulness keeps them in their rooms most of the time. This, I have found to be very common in most world big cities like New York, Rome and Tokyo.

Living in the here and now, which I call the real

world, reduces risks of possible neurotic shunts. It can also cure one of such characteristics. Becoming more free in one area in life can overlap beneficially into others. That is one of the reasons the patients of successful psycho therapy benefit from the dollars and time investment they make it themselves. All successful therapy results in the well patient always making more money, and living longer, and with more quality of life, than would, or could be the case otherwise.

The clarity and impact of past and future can be increased by living with a "today is now" attitude. The loss or lack of an adequate self-defense mechanism constricts and diminishes the functions of all organisms and societies in all times.

All living human beings are either growing or regressing. This is the reason that I believe learning and excellence are an ever on going thing in the lives of all of us. I also conclude that the body matures much more rapidly than the mind. Super normalcy in anything must be nurtured to be maintained. Poor nutrition, mentally, physically, and spiritually, affects regression. I am glad that the mind forgets pain at a greater rate than it remembers pleasure. Arthritis sufferers are able to cope with their pain because of this.

I believe that unpleasant emotions, such as fear and

anger tend to reject contact with the reality of their causative factors. This may be part of our intrinsic makeup. Senile people do not know it when they become senile. Fat people do not know it when they become fat. Lazy people do not know that they succumb to "the bubonic laziness."

Pleasure is contact with non-injurious realities. It should cause harmfulness at the moment of involvement. Involvement itself, is necessary for total contact. My own repetition of my teachings has developed many theories and systems for me about my behavior and my students' behavior. Networks of systems that evolve from collections of various Karate teachers' experiences in coping with the same given reality, make the best reference sources.

In finally putting this book to paper, I have found that involvement, itself, indicated a reason. I cite my phrase, "Sometimes, never say sometimes," as an example of the exception for proving the rule that neurosis is any consistency. Change and growth are constants in life because they are not rigid. The ability to change oneself is a non-neurotic blessing. I like to call the inevitability of change a paradox within an enigma.

Non-neurotic behavior allows for energy conversation and the ability to harness present energy. Mental health is wealth every time it happens. It must be nurtured. Prayer, or self-hypnosis, is a tool for it. It is good to remember that a shepherd will pray, not for the sheep, but rather, for the accuracy of his aim against the wolf. Sheep do not pray. Sheep do not worry, plan, save, prepare, insure against, study for anything. Prayer is a work feeling. Saving is a form of prayer.

Courage is a form of harnessed potential energy. The universe had no origins, because nothing was ever stationary. Faith is needed to see the present. The ability to have faith in a future potential is what gives us our humanity. What with "Star Wars" and other such extensions of ourselves, who knows what comes next for us. We can only guess with educated sincerity for now.

"May the force be with you," is the modern verbiage for "God bless you." I use the term "nowhereness," as slang, to describe the absence of faith in anything. That is the essence of the "depression mood." Religion, in the absence of faith, is faith in something itself. My Karate katas teach one to avoid psychological switching, or shunts, in the face of facing violent realities.

Changes in the inside world, enable changes to occur in the outside world, and vice-versa. I am overjoyed at the human potential for "spontaneous remission." Faith in a super normal potential is necessary for this to happen. Faith healings are an excellent example of this idea.

The esoteric cause for the development of Karate therapy was to change subconscious behavior. Faith is a form of confidence. One's own self-defense mechanism implies a faith in the self. Hard work must be rewarded to be motivated to continue. A pathological subconscious is a network of neurotic shunts in the psychological subconscious self-defense mechanism, in short, I call that whole thing plain ol' "ostrich-ism."

It was no fun having cured so many students through the years of disorientation, dis-association and even rigid constrictions. I did for nothing what money couldn't buy for them. There were about thirty such cases in my life. I accidentally stumbled upon the realization, in about my first ten year period as a professional Sensei of Karate, that it, itself was really one big therapy for everyone involved in it. That is why the old masters called it a way of life. Gichin Funakoshi (founder of Japan Karate), was certainly way ahead of his time during his day.

The "accuracy wall" in my old dojo was the very best tool I ever invented for teaching implicit behavior with. It is the non-pathological subconscious that deals with punching a person in the face as a lovely example of itself. It is easily understood in all times and cultures. Voodoo itself, as exhibited by my "Wanda" case history, is an example of neurotic behavior.

My use of the term CW in the "Yolanda" case history, brings out the psychology of people who rely on CW behavior. My CW (continuous waive) abbreviation is a form of spicing things up by its very use. Words are as good as perfume, music, lighting and colorations are for getting attention.

Anything accurate is capable of being measured or mathematically manipulated. Neurotics of necessity, see their world as an accurate one. We have all taken our fantasies that way sometimes. Theater people and Karate people are prone to too much of that at certain glory times in their lives. It ends when they become matured. Good Karate psychology should get all of us to adjust any super man or wonder woman complexes that we are prone to, to change to a "super normal person reality" for ourselves. Self education has the same importance in our lives that self love or self preservation does.

My Karate therapy best falls into the category of philosophical psychoanalysis of my students within the discipline of classical and scientific Karate training. In it, I refer to mathematics as a mastery that says there are no mysteries. "Changing the subject" is a form of behavior that can adequately be called a shunt, or a neurotic action. It literally terminates in itself without a resolution to the original premise.

Changing the subject when one is confused, is not part of the general problem solving process. Incomplete perception is the main cause of shunting. I spot this in my students and myself whenever we exhibit excess-emotionality. Depression is a form of excess-emotionality. It usually accompanies the illogical structure through which neurotic behavior necessarily views the accurate world. Romantic love causes a great deal of shunting in adolescent behavior. One can function much better when one sees love as an emotion and not as a divine happening. I call puppy love the classical slang term for such divine happenings.

Some of my students had Bruce Lee intoxication. I brought out to them that worshiping the artist above the art is neurotic. It is seen that way by me because, it of necessity assumes the part to be greater than the whole of a thing. Hero worship is a form of masturbatory groupie-ism. Worship itself, allows for only a one way viewpoint. Understanding is broader than worshiping Understanding is the highest form of worship I know of.

Neurotics, such as depicted in my memories of Susan's case history, manifest a stubborn insistence on pushing their behavioral modes on others. It usually depends on their willingness to allow themselves to be pushed on, or have that particular thing pushed on them. We have all dealt with many "Susan" type personalities in our lives, and now with the Guiana incident and cult awareness in our newspapers, the reality of individual shunting and group shunting become more evident to us.

Karate training, or what I call, "learning how to fight real good," explodes the myth of dominance by virtue or size inequality in people and animals.

Neurotics want someone else to be their hero and rescue them from themselves. That is the essence of my whole report to you dear reader. Neurotics attract and breed other neurotics. Any human who becomes aware of his or her neurosis, loses half of it immediately. The rest is simply a matter of following your inner voice.

Karate training must be applied from within to avoid the predicament of expecting the knowledge to do something for you in itself. We do something with the knowledge! You control the book! The book doesn't control you! These admonitions apply to our destinies too. Any therapy is complete when the patient no longer needs the therapist. Never forget that the object of therapy or teaching is to successfully complete the original premise and go to the next endeavor in work. If the patient goes on to the next therapist, the therapy has failed. Nothing else is valid.

UNIVERSAL LEADERSHIP CODE:

They who are loved too much get raped!

Those who are feared too much get killed!

But whosoever is respected...... gets things done!

THE TEN COMMANDMENTS OF GOJU

(1)
We are proud to be Martial Artists.
(2)
We shall always practice and study.
(3)
We shall always be quick to seize opportunity.
(4)
We shall always block soft and hit hard.
(5)
We shall always be persons of quality.
(6)
We shall always respect the laws of reality.
(7)
We shall always be prepared for life and death.
(8)
We shall always love our parents, teachers and family.
(9)
We shall always be true to ourselves, Martial Arts and country.
(10)
We shall always plan our work and work our plan.

Remember: It is the professional duty of a true teacher to point accurately. It is the duty of the student, to himself or herself, to do implicitly.

THE RULES OF CLASSICAL DOJOS
(1)
Everyone works!
(2)
Nothing is free!
(3)
All start at the bottom!
(4)
The Sensei's word is law
by consent of the governed!

Remember: A western philosopher once said: "From either extreme, the middle looks like the extreme."

Super-normal (chi) is often taken by our minds to be miraculous, or magically superior.

It is not!

The distance from sub-standard to normal seems magical to the sub-standard. You can imagine what super-normal must seem like to the sub-standard view.

All of us feel that way about everything we can't do until we have done it. It then becomes normal to the doers (implicit actionists), and magically superior to the normals and sub-standards. This is why hero worship exists.

Mathematics and mathematically manipulated things seem magical to me. This is because I am in awe of the power of mathematics. I am in awe because I know nothing about it. Mathematicians are in awe of karate abilities for the same reason.

My Karate philosophy views a glass of water as half full by knowing the history of the "direction" of the water. If the researched history shows that it was last poured, it is then half empty to me. When the history proves that it was last poured into, it is then half full. When there is no way to establish the history of the direction of the water, not the glass, it is then logical for me assume it is half empty because direction is always out. Direction, direction, direction is everything. Don't forget that about anything.

WE BELIEVE IN TRUTH, JUSTICE
AND THE GOJU KARATE WAY =
OUR CREED.

THE GENERAL PROBLEM SOLVING PROCESS

(1)
Define the problem!
(2)
Analyze the problem!
(3)
Search for possible solutions!
(4)
Evaluate your alternatives!
(5)
Follow your inner voice!
(6)
Work and keep thinking!
(7)
Stick to the original premise!
(8)
Return to the original premise!
(9)
Finish the original premise!
(10)
Plan your attack on the next problem!

KEEP PUNCHING!

THE GENERAL PROBLEM CAUSING PROCESS

The G.P.C.P. is simply utilizing any one or more of the following factors.

(1)
Shunting!
(2)
Occupying occupied space.
(3)
Inaccurate communications.
(4)
Lies, imaginary restrictions and unnecessary work.
(5)
Poverty, pain, temperature and hunger.
(6)
Guessing!
(7)
Erroneous physics, logic or math.
(8)
The lack of a belief in a future potential.
(9)
An inaccurate superiority complex.
(10)
An inaccurate inferiority complex.

Remember: When one or more of the factors listed enters the configuration of your observation and or evaluation of any problem or situation, immediately assume the negative side of "Murphy's Law" to be quite accurate: to wit, "If anything can go wrong, it will!"

Do not forget the converse, "If anything can go right, it will."

It is the direction of events that determines whether a thing goes right or wrong. In the accurate world there is no bending of the rules of reality. For example, water will either freeze or thaw at thirty two degrees fahrenheit. That is quite true. I can always tell what will happen by knowing the temperature right before. If the temperature is above the freezing mark to begin with and you bring it down to the freezing mark, the water will continue going in the direction of the freezing process. If the water was colder than the freezing temperature, the direction of result will be a continuation in the thawing direction.

If the physics is perfect for a thing to happen, it will. Its direction, (positive or negative) (good or bad) (yin or yang) (hard or soft) (long or short) ad infinitum, is determined by the direction it was headed in at the instance before that moment in time. Honesty is the physics of human relationships. Perfection is no accident.

May the force be with you and your plans always.

THE END...............